THE POLICE OFFICER'S GUIDE TO K9 SEARCHES

K9 Professional Training Series

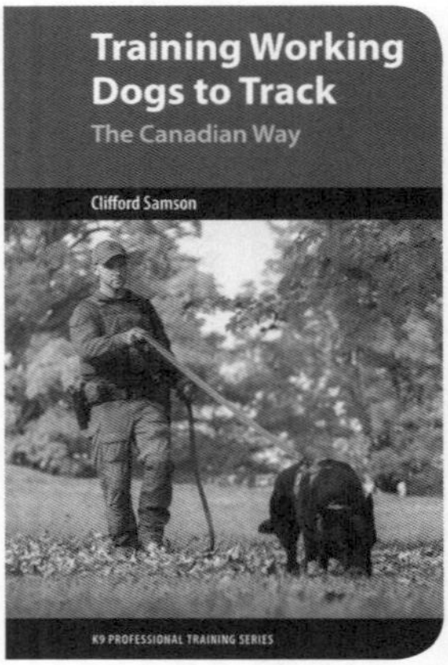

See the complete list at

dogtrainingpress.com

THE POLICE OFFICER'S GUIDE TO K9 SEARCHES

Second Edition

Stephen A. Mackenzie

R.S. Eden

K9 Professional Training Series

DOG TRAINING PRESS

An imprint of
Brush Education Inc.

Printed and manufactured in China

25 26 27 28 29 5 4 3 2 1

This book is available in print, PDF, and Global Certified Accessible™ EPUB formats.

Brush Education Inc.
www.brusheducation.ca
contact@brusheducation.ca

Brush Education is located in amiskwaciwâskahikan, Edmonton, Alberta, within Treaty 6 territory and Métis Nation of Alberta District 10, and on the traditional and ancestral territories of the Nêhiyawak, Denesuliné, Nakota Sioux, and Saulteaux Peoples.

Cover and book design: Carol Dragich, Dragich Design; Cover image: © Billy Sawyer

Photographs: © Robert S. Eden unless otherwise specified in text

Illustrations: © Natasha Serena Eden and Natasha Eden

Library and Archives Canada Cataloguing in Publication

Title: The police officer's guide to K9 searches / Stephen A. Mackenzie, R.S. Eden.
Names: Mackenzie, Stephen Alexander, author | Eden, R. S. (Robert S.), author
Description: Second edition. | Includes index.
Identifiers: Canadiana (print) 2025013635X | Canadiana (ebook) 20250136368 | ISBN 9781550599237 (softcover) | ISBN 9781550599244 (PDF) | ISBN 9781550599251 (EPUB)
Subjects: LCSH: Police dogs. | LCSH: Search dogs. | LCSH: Tracking dogs. | LCSH: Detector dogs. | LCSH: Searches and seizures—Canada.
Classification: LCC HV8025 .M323 2025 | DDC 363.28—dc23

We acknowledge the support of the Government of Canada
Nous reconnaissons l'appui du gouvernement du Canada | Canada

For Laurie, Dawn, and Alex.

Contents

Preface

New police officers have a large number of tools to master in order to become efficient at their work. From computers to portable radar, the number of technical devices needed and used by the modern police officer is constantly growing, and one of the more mysterious and poorly understood tools at an officer's disposal is the police service dog. Even experienced officers need to be occasionally reminded about when, and why, to call for the K9 unit. So, whether you are an instructor exposing academy recruits to the tools of modern police work or an experienced officer wishing to have a quick reference to consult, every officer should have something that explains how police dogs work, what operations they can help you with, and how you can support them during their deployments. This book is an attempt to fill that need.

DISCLAIMER

Part I

A Police Officer's Introduction to K9 Searches

1

What Is a Police Service Dog?

Every line officer needs to understand the versatility of police service dog teams and be aware of how to best work with those teams. Police service dogs are an effective resource at your disposal when pursuing fleeing suspects, locating and recovering evidence at crime scenes, or searching for stolen property, contraband, or explosive devices. They can be a primary tool of de-escalation in situations involving armed and dangerous persons.

Deployment of the K9 unit is a team effort. This cannot be stressed enough. Patrol officers are as important to the successful application of the dog as the dog team itself. Without proper backup, containment, and scene preservation by patrol officers, the chances for a successful conclusion to any K9 application are reduced. When officers properly contain and preserve a scene, the K9 team's success rate can increase as much as 30 to 40 percent.

Defining police service dogs

Police service dog is a general term that is used to refer to any dog trained for and used in any aspect of police work. Police service dogs may also be called *utility dogs* or *patrol dogs*.

Officer Shelby Wright of the Lakewood Police Department (Colorado) trains with police service dog Loki. © Krista Schmit

Many, but not all, police service dogs have some kind of aggression or bite training geared toward handler protection and/or suspect apprehension. This is an important aspect of the utility of police service dogs, and we will touch on it in this book, but is not the book's focus. We will focus instead on how police service dogs can be deployed to assist in police searches.

Police service dogs may be trained in one or several different search techniques including tracking, trailing, area searches, building searches, and article (evidence) searches. Insofar as they search for living human beings and the things those human beings have touched, the function of police service dogs overlaps with search-and-rescue dogs. However, police service dogs may also be trained in a detection profile geared toward nonhuman scents, such as narcotics or explosives.

Police service dogs can be single purpose or dual purpose. Single-purpose dogs are trained in one search skillset only: for instance, detecting narcotics or tracking suspects. Dual-purpose dogs may be trained in a number of different skill sets. These could include a combination of one or more suspect search techniques, a detection profile, and, in many cases, handler protection and suspect apprehension. The dogs in any K9 unit will have different training profiles.

Make sure you know the tasks the dogs in your area are trained for so you can call for the appropriate dog at the appropriate time.

Even when you are working with a dog that is trained in only one search technique, it is important to note that search dogs naturally use several different techniques to follow scents. In police and search-and-rescue contexts, we tend to separate these into three categories: tracking, trailing, and area searching or air scenting. While these strategies do have distinct differences, officers should recognize that most dogs will be trained in more than one search strategy, and that these strategies have a lot of cross-over. For instance, while a tracking dog primarily follows scent close to the ground, it will begin to follow air scent as it nears the person it's looking for because that person's scent is floating on air currents. We'll get into the details of different search techniques later in the book. For now, suffice it to say that tracking, trailing, and air-scenting dogs are all search dogs, and they will search with whatever means they have available to them.

Why call for police service dogs?

The primary purpose of a police dog is the application of its olfactory capabilities to search for someone or something that is difficult to find. Officers are frequently faced with these situations. Sometimes they are looking for a person who is lost or actively fleeing a crime. Other times they are looking for evidence that a suspect has dropped in or around the scene of a crime. Still other times, they are trying to determine the location, or perhaps even the presence, of a contraband substance or an explosive device. These are all ideal situations for calling in a police service dog.

Many officers have the mistaken impression that the primary purpose of a police service dog is to be used as a use-of-force tool. While it is true that dogs can and do bite people when required, this is far from their primary application. In fact, police dog deployments, even during active searches for criminal suspects or crimes in progress, result in bites on suspects less than 10 percent of the time. The other 90 percent of a dog's work involves its nose.

In fact, some agencies do not train their patrol dogs in aggression at all to ensure that the dog never engages—that is, bites—a missing person, regardless of what that person does. These agencies believe that this will decrease liability for the officers and agency while still providing efficient searches.

The flip side of having a dog that is not trained in criminal apprehension is that it makes searches for potentially armed and/or dangerous suspects more hazardous for officers involved in such searches.

The bottom line is this: while the possibility of deploying a dog as a use-of-force tool is an important asset when needed, the average officer should understand and use the police service dog as an investigative tool whose primary function is the use of its olfactory capabilities to locate people, evidence, and contraband.

How do police service dogs search?

For thousands of years, through evolution, dogs have been masters of searching for and finding things. The natural, biological desire to hunt (search) has been maintained and nurtured by breeders and trainers of working dogs. These natural desires, along with a number of other factors (which we will get into later in this chapter), push dogs to incredible performance levels that far outmatch human capability and contribute to the enormous value that dogs have as investigative tools.

However, a desire to hunt does not on its own necessarily make a dog good at finding what it's looking for. This skill is attributable to another biological factor: the dog's nose. We human beings rely largely on our eyes to search for people and things that are difficult to find. While this can certainly be an effective method, it has its drawbacks. For one, it can be quite inefficient. For another, we may miss important clues or information. We simply can't see what we can't see. The acuity of a dog's nose is what gives it the ability to efficiently detect and follow an odor, and often find or indicate the odor's source, even when that source is unreachable or invisible to us. Suspects can be hidden, as can contraband items, but the odor signature that these emit is nearly impossible to contain, and it is this emanating odor that the dogs are able to work with and focus on.

THE CANINE SENSE OF SMELL

If we were to look closely at the inner structure of a dog's nose, we would see a maze of tiny, scroll-like passages along the nasal septum. These passages are actually made up of small, membrane-covered bones called the turbinate bones. Toward the back of the nose, the membranes covering the turbinate bones are full of scent receptor cells.

Human noses also have turbinate bones and, of course, scent receptors—yet dog are many times more sensitive to odors than human, in part because they simply have many more scent receptors in their noses than we do.

Dogs also have a scent-receptor-covered gland in the roof of the mouth, between the upper canine teeth, called the vomeronasal gland. This gland gives dogs the ability to detect any odor that is drawn in through the mouth. In police dog applications it helps the dog to track a fresh scent very rapidly by taking odor in through the mouth as well as the nose.

ODOR DETECTION AND ALERTS

All dogs have a powerful ability to detect and analyze odors. They also have an innate ability to store and recall odors that they have imprinted in their memories. Police service dogs are conditioned to use those abilities to detect specific odors, even when the source of those odors can't be seen or an odor is present in very small amounts.

Police service dogs are also trained to indicate the presence of their target odor or odors. They will follow an odor trail to the point where it is strongest, most often the source of the target odor. (There are exceptions to this, such as in cases of suspects hiding in locations that create occurrences such as the "chimney effect" which will be discussed later.) As the dog approaches this point, and the target odor becomes stronger, you may see behavior changes such as the dog lifting its head and beginning to work the odor through its mouth. At the same time, the dog will become more excited and search with more intensity, often increasing in pace. This is a significant change of behavior. When handlers see this change of behavior, they will interpret this as a strong indicator that the dog is closing in on the source of the odor it is looking for. If the source of that odor is a suspect, the handler and backup officers should prepare for a possible confrontation.

In situations such as narcotics detection, a dog will exhibit a similar natural change of behavior when it detects a trained odor. When the dog finds the point where the odor is strongest, it will indicate that it has located the strongest source of odor by sitting and staring intently at where it believes the contraband to be, or scratching at where it believes the source of the odor is secreted. Current training preferences will normally be what is referred to as a passive response, which is the dog sitting as a final indication, often referred to as a final response. For the purposes of this book, any behavior that indicates to the handler that the dog has found its intended target we will refer to as a *final response behavior* or *indication*. When a handler perceives that their dog has detected a target odor, they will call an *alert*. Note, however, that terminology may vary from one jurisdiction to the next. It is therefore wise to check definitions when discussing police service dog searches with someone from a different jurisdiction.

Dogs have different behaviors that indicate they have detected a target odor, depending on the situation and how the dog is trained to respond. To be a true final response behavior, a dog's behavior must satisfy three conditions. First, the dog's behavior must change significantly as it works the odor. Second, the dog must exhibit its trained final response behavior, showing that it thinks it has done well enough to earn a reward. (An exception will be situations where the dog is not in a position to exhibit its trained final response.) Third, the handler has to be satisfied enough with the dog's behavior to call the alert. Ultimately, everything depends on how the handler reads the dog. It should also be noted that in circumstances where a dog may not be able to perform its specifically trained response, certain changes in its behavior will still make it very clear to the dog handler that the dog is sensing what it is looking for.

We will discuss alerts and changes of behavior further in chapter 6. For the time being, remember that the handler will know when the dog's behavior indicates the presence of a scent or odor, whether or not the dog has performed a formal final response behavior.

Police dogs as investigative tools

We'll say it again: police service dogs are incredible investigative tools. This, more than anything else, is the reason that all departments should have access to K9 services.

But what, exactly, do we mean when we say that police service dogs are an investigative tool? Most obviously, as we've already explored, dogs' sense of smell allows them to find many things that their human counterparts will miss. However, simply finding things is not the be all, end all of an investigation.

Whether a police service dog finds what you are looking for or not, it will give you more information about the situation you are investigating than you had before deploying the dog. This ability to provide information even when they don't appear to complete their task is what makes dogs such wonderful investigative tools.

Officer Erik Good and his K9 of the Fort Lauderdale Police work a track in an outdoor, urban area at night. © Erik Good, Fort Lauderdale Police

Let's look at some examples. Say you are looking for a suspect who has fled a crime scene. Even if the dog is unable to locate the suspect, it is likely to be able to tell you what direction the suspect traveled in if the suspect left on foot. This type of information has proven very helpful to real-life investigations. Police dog information was used to solve one series of thefts when the directions of the incomplete tracks from all the scenes pointed to one residential section of a city. Surveillance was set up, and soon the individual was apprehended coming home after his latest break-in, stolen property in hand.

In other situations, dogs will track to a location on a street and lose the track completely. When this happens, good investigators know enough to start interviewing nearby residents to see if anyone saw a person get into a vehicle at that spot at the appropriate time. They often get a description of the individual they were tracking, the type of vehicle the person got into, and the direction in which they were headed when they left. Of course, sometimes there are no witnesses. Maybe a suspect got into a vehicle on an abandoned road. Even in these cases, a police dog can help you by finding incriminating evidence along the track that you weren't specifically looking for—perhaps something that can provide DNA or positive fingerprint matches. You now have a key piece of physical evidence you would have missed if you hadn't had a search dog with you to follow the track.

Sometimes, a police dog may fail to find any track at all. In one case of alleged sexual assault, for example, the female victim claimed she had been sexually assaulted in her home and that the perpetrator had exited the house out a back window and fled through the back yard. Attending officers sealed off the area and called in a police service dog, however the dog could not find a track. Subsequent to deploying the dog, the handler informed the investigators of what the dog found—or rather, didn't find: that there was no indication of anyone having been in the back yard. Trusting this information, investigators challenged the complainant about the allegation. Faced with the fact that the dog had found no evidence to support her original story, she eventually admitted that no sexual assault had occurred. She had made the call in an attempt to get the attention of her boyfriend, who she felt had been losing interest in her.

The list could go on, but the point should by now be clear: dogs do not have to find what they start out searching for in order to be valuable to a police investigation. Whether or not a dog finds what it was originally brought in to find, good investigators use the information dog teams provide to add to the pieces of the puzzle they must solve.

K9 evidence recovery

Police officers spend a good percentage of their careers searching for evidence to aid in the prosecution of the suspects they arrest. In search-and-rescue work, we will also be interested in anything the person discarded. These things can give us information about their direction of travel, insight into their mental state, how serious their situation is, and more. The items can end up being vital evidence.

Evidence recovery is a skill that most standard patrol or utility dogs are trained for, alongside skills such as tracking, trailing, area search, detection, and others. When K9 handlers use their dogs to recover evidence, they deploy them on what is often referred to as an "article search." Dogs can search an area for items faster and more accurately than any group of humans because of their acute olfactory ability. They will find items more efficiently than their human colleagues, even when those colleagues walk their search grids shoulder to shoulder. Using a dog to search an area for potential evidence or discarded articles and can significantly reduce the time required to cover the search area.

Dogs working article searches recover evidence in much the same manner that they search for and find people in area searches, but the articles dogs are searching for may be any size: for example, dogs are very capable of searching for and locating articles as small as a discarded shell casing from a fired bullet or a discarded wallet or purse. They are, however, equally useful in locating bigger articles such as a rifle hidden under tangled foliage. Dogs can be trained to use their air-scenting abilities to locate any object that has human odor on it and is within the search area, and they will also key in on objects that are not natural to the surrounding area. For example, a brass shell casing will give off a distinct odor that is different from the natural surroundings and will easily be detected by a well-trained dog. Any situation in which there is a possibility for recovering discarded evidence provides an opportunity for the application of a dog trained in evidence recovery. Evidence often makes or breaks a case, and the use of a police dog to search for articles and recover evidence greatly increases your chances of success.

WORKING WITH DOGS DEPLOYED ON ARTICLE SEARCHES

When working with a dog that is deployed to find evidence, it's important to remember your basic responsibilities. Handlers will begin the search on the downwind side of the search area and allow the dog to vector into the wind to give it the best chance of detecting any scent that may be emanating from discarded articles. When an area is determined to potentially contain items that are of evidentiary value, it is important to preserve the area. Remember that a dog searching for articles is searching for a smaller amount of human odor than it would be if it were searching for a person. Although dogs can work through substantial amounts of contamination, it is always wise to keep the area secure to limit further contamination: the less human contamination there is in the search area the better.

If deemed necessary, a grid search by human searchers may be done after the dog team has cleared the area.

Other advantages of K9 searches

Police service dogs have numerous traits that allow them to maximize their information-finding ability and provide their human colleagues with an edge in their searches.

For example, because dogs can search so precisely and efficiently, they can reduce the time needed for investigative follow-up by detectives. More than this, searches involving police service dogs require fewer personnel and thus contribute to significant savings in personnel hours. This in turn frees up officers for other responsibilities.[1]

Dogs are also eager to work regardless of the time of day. They are just as eager to perform when you wake them up in the middle of the night as they are during their day shift. They don't care if it is vacation time or a holiday. In some respects, they are the perfect employees: they always want to work.

Dogs are extremely thorough searchers. They make no assumptions about where things or people can or can't be—something human personnel are famous for. Human officers often neglect to effectively search certain parts of a search area because they are convinced in their minds that the person or object they are searching for could not possibly be there. Dogs make no such assumptions.

Dogs also do not have to see things to find them. Their noses give them the ability to search areas they cannot see into. Police dogs do not have to open doors to know what's behind them. This is especially useful in searching for hidden explosives and avoiding booby traps. Dogs can also use their noses to search effectively in the dark without the need for flashlights—a major tactical advantage. Due to the way odor drifts, dogs can often detect who or what they are looking for from a significant distance, then zero in on the source location. In searches for hidden assailants, police dogs can not only detect the suspect well in advance, but also indicate with a natural change of behavior when the team is approaching a suspect, alerting the team before the suspect is able to ambush them.

Unlike their human colleagues, dogs are not worried about getting their uniform dirty or torn. It is continually amazing how much influence the condition of a human officer's uniform has on their mental processes during a search. Of course, looking sharp and professional is necessary in police work. For some officers, however, that mental need to keep the uniform clean works against them during

1 R.S. Eden, *K9 Supervisor's Manual* (Edmonton: Dog Training Press, 2021), pp. 4–8. This section of *Supervisor's Manual* cites a 1990s study on the effectiveness of police dogs conducted by Officer Marie Wolfe of the Lansing Police Department in Michigan. Officer Wolfe's study was never published but was widely circulated at the time.

searches. They may skip over certain parts of the search area solely to preserve their uniforms. A dedicated dog team has no such concern. The dog in particular will go to any length to attain its goal, regardless of conditions.

In a similar vein, dogs are not discouraged by difficult terrain. It is not unusual for officers to be on their hands and knees crawling through brambles and briars for hours to search an area (particularly if evidence has been discarded by a suspect in such an area). This is also an issue when criminals who do not wish to be located deliberately go into difficult areas knowing it will be challenging for officers to follow them. Without a K9 team, this tactic is frequently successful for suspects. Even if not concerned with their uniforms, officers may become discouraged, fail to search an area effectively, or simply give up the chase in extremely adverse terrain. Police dogs have more staying power in these situations. They will eagerly tackle difficult terrain and search effectively regardless of the lay of the land.

Dogs can search in other difficult environments, as well. For instance, they can work effectively in tear gas environments. Dogs are better at flushing the irritants in CS and OC (pepper spray) out of their eyes and nose than humans are. Their bodies are alkaline by nature, which helps to counteract the acidic nature of gas and they also have a built-in defense for the eyes called a nictitating membrane. This membrane is translucent and is often referred to as a third eyelid. When the eyes are irritated, that membrane slides up over the eye to help shield it, thus adding another layer of protection against irritant gases. With proper exposure in training, dogs are able to withstand these environments quite well. While we try not to work dogs for too long in these environments, this makes a police service dog team very useful in tactical situations that involve searching for and locating hidden suspects during potentially dangerous operations where gas is deployed.

Finally, when a search succeeds in locating a person—especially when that person is a potentially dangerous suspect—dogs can be effective distraction and de-escalation tools. When suspects realize they are being searched for by a police dog, it puts significant mental pressure on fleeing suspects. This results in the perpetrator often making mistakes and exposing themselves or even surrendering to officers that are set up for containment. Captured suspects often claim that they could think of little else except getting away from the dog.

Experienced K9 handlers can probably add to this list, but the point should by now be clear. Police dogs offer so many advantages that unless there are strong reasons for *not* using them, officers should call for K9 services whenever they have a search that is appropriate for them.

This, of course, brings up the question: What type of searches are appropriate for K9 teams? This is an excellent question, and one that the rest of this book attempts to define. Before we jump into that question, though, let's take a look at some basic responsibilities and considerations to keep in mind as a police officer working with K9 teams.

Things to remember when working with K9 teams

The most important thing for any officer providing support to a K9 team is to ask the handler what support they need. While most K9 teams deploy in a similar manner, every K9 team will have its own routine in how it approaches each deployment. Handlers know best what they and their dogs need to do their job most effectively. That being said, there are a few general considerations to keep in mind that will apply in most K9 search situations.

A K9 team works a search on line. © Billy Sawyer

First, remember that police service dogs are dogs. They are living creatures, and like all living beings, they have certain biological needs that need to be met. This is as true for an off-duty dog as it is for an on-duty dog. For a police service dog to do its job well, it must, in particular, be given the time to relieve itself and to drink water. As such, depending on how busy the team has been, and whether they have had any chance to allow for breaks in between calls, the handler may take a short minute to provide time for the dog to look after these needs. Allowing for this time may be frustrating for an officer on duty, especially in situations where time is of the essence. However, it is an important step in the success of the search. The dog will search much more effectively if it is not distracted by internal discomfort and when its nose is moist.

Second, understand that handlers are responsible for the safety of their dogs. They will not bring their dog into a search area unless that area is safe and secure. In some cases, officers can improve the safety of a search by providing proper scene containment and effective backup. In other cases, an area's safety depends on factors that are outside the officers' control. For instance, if a dog team is responding to the scene of a burglary in progress where the front windows have been smashed and interior display cases have been broken leaving extensive amounts of shattered glass on the ground, the handler will need to assess whether or not the dog can be deployed safely. In some cases, they may have protective boots that their dogs have been trained to wear and work in, and will need time to properly equip the dog before it can work in certain environments. Having said that, not all agencies provide such gear, and it may not be available.

If the handler decides an area or situation is unsafe for themselves or the dog, they may refuse to deploy the dog. This is part of their job, and their decision must be respected. Another example is the use of the dog in a situation such as a potentially armed confrontation. The handler will know the limitations of his or her dog and in such circumstances, will ultimately always have the final say on whether the dog will be deployed. It is vital to understand that sending a dog in to apprehend a known armed suspect is generally extremely unwise and should only be done under extreme circumstances. Even then, appropriate distraction devices and other techniques and tactics can be used alongside the dog to enhance its safety whenever possible. In most cases, the use of a dog to directly apprehend an armed suspect should be a last resort.

Third, once a search does begin, expect the K9 handler to be very particular—even fanatical—about maintaining their search pattern. If the dog is searching for odor carried through the air, know that the handler will often insist on beginning the search on the downwind side of the search area, wherever that happens to be, and regardless of where the suspect was last seen. Doing so makes it easier to present all possible air flow options to the dog. As a supporting officer, it is important for you to remember that the K9 handler is not just trying to be difficult; maintaining their search pattern is an important part of their job. It is your job to either stay out of their way or help them preserve and complete their search pattern. Again, ask the handler for direction and follow their instructions to the best of your ability.

Fourth, trust the police service dog's abilities and K9 handler's expertise when it comes to interpreting the dog's behavior. Understand that dogs indicate odors, not necessarily the source of odors. This can lead to some behavior on the part of the dog that may, to the uninitiated, appear odd or mistaken—for instance, a dog failing to find a track at all, suddenly losing a track that it had been following, or indicating at a blank wall. Trust the handler's interpretations of these behaviors, and remember that any information a dog gives you in a search is valuable. As long as the dog gives you more information than you had before, their search has been a success.

Finally, dogs are animals, not machines. While extremely rare, they occasionally have bad days. Like us, they can simply shut down and stop working due to illness, heat exhaustion, or other unknown factors. Handlers will recognize when their dog is struggling in these ways and will either stop to let the dog have a rest or abort their search. This should not cause you to lose faith in the dog, the handler, or their abilities. A bad day does not make a dog bad or unreliable. We all have bad days, and all things considered, dogs have far fewer of them than people do.

2

K9 Search Basics for Police Officers

Dogs are an invaluable addition to a search team looking for a missing person or suspect or searching for contraband, explosives, or other substances. However, officers need to understand that dogs are not a golden ticket to a successful search. When working with a K9 search team, police officers need to remain alert and active, and understand their responsibilities before, during, and after the search. Depending on the situation, these responsibilities may include assessing, containing, and preserving the scene; applying an understanding of common suspect behaviors; and using solid general and K9-specific tactical strategies when backing up your K9 team and bringing a suspect into custody.

Preserving the scene

Good scene preservation is an important aspect of any investigation but has particular significance when it comes to working with K9 teams, whether a search involves an actively fleeing suspect or not: to keep other people, whether on foot or in vehicles, from entering the area being searched. This is both for their own safety and to prevent them from adding more odor to the area in which the dog has to work. In effect, you are preserving the scene. The less odor contamination, the better the dog will search.

Contamination can come from vehicles as much as from foot traffic. Do not hesitate to stop cars from driving over a road the suspects are likely to have crossed. This will prevent cars from driving over any possible track left by the suspect. Officers should also be aware that exhaust from cars, especially those equipped with catalytic converters, is particularly detrimental to the dog's sense of smell. It has a numbing effect on the dog's olfactory system. Although it is only a brief hindrance, it can mean the difference between a successful and unsuccessful start to a deployment. Whenever you are parked near where the dog team is working, shut down your engine until the dog is away from the vehicle.

If it has been decided that a dog will be beneficial to the investigation, it is important to note that preservation of the scene also means that officers need to limit their own movement within an area and do minimal onsite investigation until after the dog has been deployed. The less contamination by on-scene officers the better.

Containment

When a search involves actively fleeing criminal suspects, containment is used to force the suspect to go to ground, or hide. When you can force a suspect to go to ground and stay in one place, this allows the K9 team time to arrive, gain ground, and begin to narrow in on the suspect.

Getting a suspect to go to ground involves interfering with their autonomic flight response. The autonomic flight response refers to a person's unconscious impulse to run without thinking. Most people in this state will exhibit a set of predictable behavior patterns, which we discuss below. When these patterns are disrupted through the obvious presence of police, it causes the suspect to stop and think about what their next move will be in order to avoid capture.

In most cases, visible police officers or patrol car lights are enough to cause this type of mental disruption. They make the suspect aware of the fact that police are in the area, and make them conscious of their surroundings. The suspect's unconscious flight pattern breaks down. Conscious thought processes are slow, and most suspects will usually respond by finding a place to hide while they try to determine their next move. Their level of fear of being found will also increase, causing them to release more stress hormones, perspire more, and exude more human odor, making it easier for the dog to detect the suspect as it closes in on location where the suspect is hiding.

DECIDING ON CONTAINMENT PERIMETERS

If the person you are looking for is trying to evade you, a perimeter should be set up as soon as possible to contain your suspects. When setting up coordinates for containment, you must always be conscious of the time delays involved. This is especially true if you are responding to a crime in progress or a fleeing suspect. If the crime is on view and reported in progress as you approach the scene, then you know you can set up your containment within a tighter perimeter. However, if you are responding to an incident that, for example, set off a silent alarm, there is a good chance the suspects will be in and out of the target area before the alarm company gets the call through to your dispatch and, in turn, to you. Your response time to the scene will determine where you set up your initial containment perimeter.

The major mistake made by officers setting up containment is setting up too close to the scene. A good rule of thumb is to give two blocks for every minute of time delay, to a maximum of six blocks from the crime scene for an initial perimeter. This can be adjusted as new information comes in, and a second containment perimeter can be set up outside the original if cars are available.

If there are not enough officers to make a complete perimeter, a partial perimeter should be set up and moved so that it is always in front of the dog's latest direction of travel. This is because when suspects hear the dog coming, they tend to keep moving ahead of the dog in the same direction as the dog team is going. So long as officers are correctly positioned at the perimeter, the suspect's movement pattern will often push them into officers on the perimeter, resulting in a successful apprehension.

Once into position, illuminate every emergency light and spotlight you have available. Let the suspect know you are there so they will not try to break through the containment.

If you feel you are at risk and exposed by staying in your patrol car, secure the vehicle and exit to a secure vantage point. For example, if you know the suspects are armed and feel you may be at risk staying in the car, set up the area you want lit up with your vehicle, and exit to a concealed location that offers good cover and where you can observe the target area and still maintain control over your vehicle.

If air support is available, make sure it is coordinated with the K9 team. Different handlers will have different preferences, but many of them want the helicopter out in front of them to encourage the suspect to go to ground. At night, a good technique to encourage suspects to go to ground is for the helicopter crew to light up the area just ahead the suspect, even if the air crew has a good visual of the suspect on FLIR (forward-looking infrared). This gives the suspect the impression that the air crew is still searching for them. The suspect will often go to ground and stay put when trying to avoid the search light of the helicopter, not realizing the crew already has them visible on FLIR, and allowing the dog team an opportunity to close ground.

UNDERSTANDING SUSPECT BEHAVIORS WHEN ELUDING ARREST

When a K9 team pursues a fleeing suspect, several environmental factors may come into play and make their job more challenging. Wind can scatter the scent. Extreme temperatures can freeze or evaporate it. Moderate to heavy rains can wash it away. Vehicular and pedestrian traffic can disturb or contaminate it. Time delays magnify these problems in some situations. Any of these factors, alone or in combination, can defeat the dog. As a result, the dog will sometimes lose the track.

When a dog loses a track, officers will need to bring in other skills and knowledge to help the dog find it again. These may include man-tracking skills as well as knowledge of criminal profiles and the typical behaviors of suspects when eluding arrest. Understanding how to assess an environment for evidence of a person in flight and how to predict a person's behaviors and decisions as they flee are assets on any search team, and to patrol officers and handlers alike. Even when there is no dog team available, patrol officers can use these skills and knowledge to recover evidence and locate fleeing suspects.

Information on suspect behaviors in pursuits is largely limited to anecdotal evidence. However, patterns have been identified within this anecdotal evidence that may be used, with caution, to guide a track.

In the 1980s, the Calgary Police Service identified several surprisingly consistent patterns in the suspect behaviors its officers had encountered during tracks. One important pattern had to do with handedness. In Calgary officers' experience, when under the stress of being pursued by police after committing a crime, suspects demonstrated significantly consistent behaviors. Officers also noticed that these consistencies may be linked to a suspect's dominant hand: right-handed people, in particular—who make up the majority of the population—tended to behave in similar ways. While anecdotal, this pattern was borne out again and again by Calgary officers' on-the-job experience, and has been noticed by many officers since then, as well. These are the most common habits we have noticed among right-handed suspects:

- A suspect exiting a doorway will usually turn to the latch side of the door.
- A suspect who runs across a residential property in order to move from a street to an alleyway (or vice versa) will usually go around the right side of the building on that property, even if the right side is obstructed and the left side is open (see figure 1).

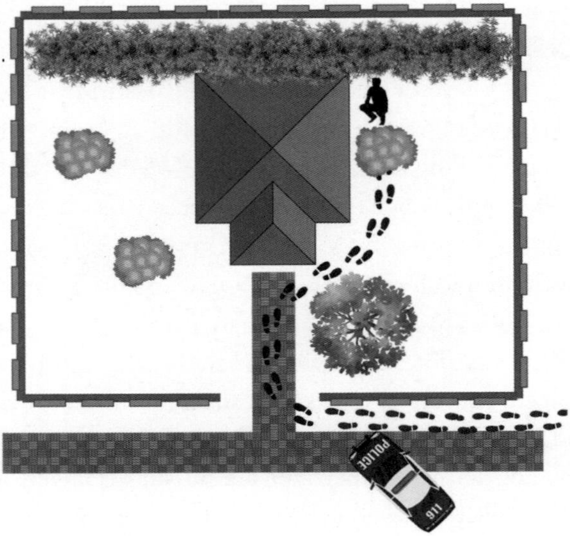

Figure 1 A suspect hiding on the right side of a building.

- When running down an alley or street, the suspect will use the right side.
- Often, when suspects are not in autonomic flight, they will only employ left turns to avoid immediate capture, or to gain some distant objective that cannot be reached by using right turns alone.
- In most cases, when a suspect is still in autonomic flight, the suspect's first turn will be to the left, followed by a series of consecutive rights before another left turn, and so on.
- When containment officers and/or a K9 team can force a suspect to use left turns, the suspect often panics and goes to ground.
- After jumping over a fence, most suspects will go left. (Most right-handed people have a tendency to lift their right leg over first, causing the body to turn to the left as they straddle the fence, naturally making them move in that direction when they dismount the other side.)
- When suspects go to ground, they will often have a tendency to hide on the right-hand side of the track. When two or more suspects flee in the same direction together, they will often go to ground within a hundred feet of one another. This can be an officer safety issue when one is found.

Understanding these behaviors can do more than help you relocate a track. They can be leveraged to force a suspect to make mistakes or go to ground, ultimately helping the dog team gain ground and locate the suspect.

Backing up your K9 team

Effective backup is vital to K9 operations. Most K9 officers who are injured or killed on duty were without a backup at the time of the confrontation. Ideally, a backup team should include backup officers who have trained with the K9 unit and know how to protect them without distracting the dog.

If you have not trained with the handler or dog, be sure to ask the handler if and how they would like you to work with them.

THE POLICE OFFICER'S ROLE

You become a part of the K9 team when you provide backup. When working as a backup to the dog unit, you must be prepared to keep up with your handler under any circumstance and remain alert to your surroundings and the situation as it develops.

Unfortunately, many officers drop out of the chase when the terrain gets challenging. They get discouraged when they must start jumping fences, or they hesitate when the area gets muddy and their uniform starts to get soiled—circumstances that may be relatively unusual to them, though they are run-of-the-mill for K9 handlers. As police officers, dress and deportment has been drilled into us from the first days in the academy. We instinctively slow down and pick our way through muddy areas to stay as clean as possible. However, this kind of hesitancy from backup officers has resulted in handlers confronting suspects on their own and even being injured or shot. Had there been a backup officer present in these situations, the outcome would likely have been significantly different.

Other officers may get distracted by the dog itself. Indeed, most people in the presence of a search dog want to watch the dog work. If a backup officer allows themselves to be distracted by the dog, they may miss potential danger signs that they may have otherwise seen. Every dog track or search has the potential to pull you and the K9 team into a potential ambush and, depending on how the air is moving at the time, it is not uncommon for the dog to overshoot and miss the suspects' location, thus putting the team in imminent danger. Remember to be a police officer first and a dog enthusiast second.

Good backup officers understand that it is the K9 handler's job, not their own, to watch the dog as it works. Good backup officers also understand that, because K9 handlers are focused on their dogs, they will be less prepared to defend themselves if the need arises. If working on lead, a handler cannot have their weapon at the ready should a confrontation suddenly occur. It is your responsibility to remain alert, scan the environment, and stay with your dog handler to be prepared to handle such a situation.

If you cannot stay focused and keep up with the physical challenges faced by the K9 team, then find another officer who can. Good backup is vital to the handler's and dog's safety and often, ultimately, their survival.

POSITIONING

Correct positioning is essential to backing up a K9 team on any search that may involve a possible confrontation.

Experience gleaned from tracking deployments indicates that most suspects conceal themselves on the right side of a track. If you are the lone backup officer, you should therefore place yourself about twenty feet behind the dog handler and about ten to twenty feet to the handler's right: the four o'clock position (figure 2). This configuration allows for an adequate spread between you and the handler to avoid being caught in a potential ambush, but is close enough that your side arm will remain effective. If you have one available, however, rifles are preferred over side arms when backing up K9 teams. They are better in the bush and allow for better accuracy and longer reach should a confrontation occur.

The four o'clock position is important as it allows you the best possibility of a clear field of fire due to the tendency for suspects to go to ground on the right side of a track. It also allows you to give adequate cover to the area in front of the handler—something that officers who backup the K9 team by positioning themselves directly behind the handler, at the six o'clock or rear-guard position, are unable to do. By using the four o'clock escort procedure, you force the suspect to deal with the dog as well as two officers—the handler and yourself—all at different angles and distances. The psychological advantage is tremendous and often causes suspects to change their minds about engaging in a gunfight.

If there are two backup officers, one should be at the four o'clock position and the other at the eight o'clock position. This allows both backup officers maximum fields of fire in both directions. In a serious situation where you have the benefit of three backup officers, the third officer can take the six o'clock or rear-guard position, about twenty feet farther behind the handler than the other two officers. Again, this provides for maximum coverage from all officers without as much concern about crossfire should the suspect decide to engage in a firefight.

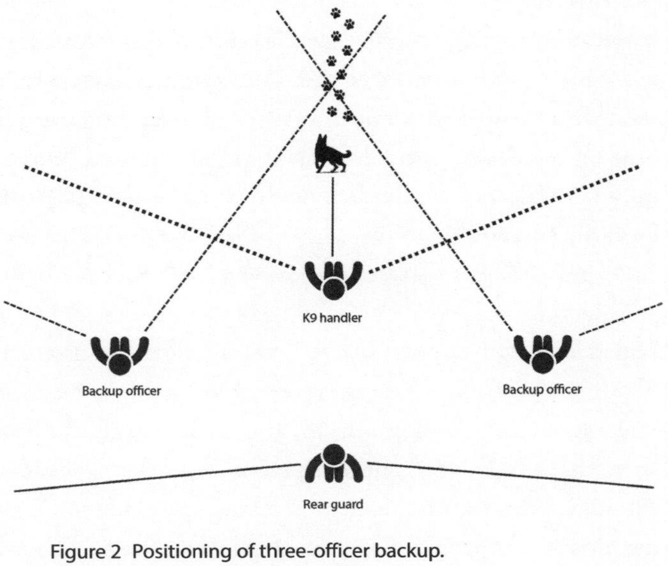

Figure 2 Positioning of three-officer backup.

Track types

Tracks left by individuals are categorized into two basic groups: passive tracks and active tracks. Note that the term *track* in this context simply refers to the trail of odor left by a person, and not to the type of search strategy that should be used by the dog. In other words, when we talk about "following a track," we are simply talking about following a path of odors to their source, whether that's using a tracking, trailing, or air-scenting technique.

Regardless of what kind of track you're dealing with, the importance of setting up and maintaining proper containment cannot be understated. For officers providing backup, it is crucial that you stay with the team to the completion of the search, whether the track is active or passive.

That being said, both types of tracks have their own characteristics and challenges. It is important that police officers know these differences, understand how they may affect the behavior of the K9 teams you work with, and are aware of the risks of each situation.

PASSIVE TRACKS

Passive tracks are tracks left by people who are not in any rush or panic, and under little or no pressure to avoid detection. These include lost persons, elderly people who walk away from homes, and even criminals who do not feel pressured by their circumstances. People who are not stressed do not exude the same type or level of pheromones that are easily perceptible to the dog as those who are under pressure to avoid capture. When a suspect is fleeing a crime scene, stress levels result in high cortisol levels in the body and significant pheromones are released with the suspects' scent. This is referred to as enhanced odor. Conversely, when searching for someone who is not excreting a lot of enhanced odor, the dog working the track may give indications similar to what a handler might interpret as a trail that is older, as the dog will not exhibit the same type of tracking excitement as if it were tracking an actively fleeing suspect who is under pressure to escape.

These people tend to also move slower and perspire less, reducing the scent picture for the dog.

This can be deceptive, and potentially dangerous, especially if the team becomes complacent during the search. As a patrol officer, remember this: just because a track is passive doesn't mean the situation is safe.

For instance, I.V. drug users frequently fall into the category of a passive track. This is not because the suspect is unaware of being pursued, but because the suspect is high and may not be terribly stressed or concerned about the situation. They are not feeling fear, so they are not exuding the typical pheromones brought on when under stress. Their body is not pumping large amounts of adrenaline and cortisol levels may be close to normal.

For the dog, this means that the human odor scent picture is different and may not be as discernable to the dog as those persons they frequently pursue on active tracks. Even as the dog closes in on the suspect, it may not give the officer the usual indications of being in close proximity to the suspect. The K9 team may therefore find themselves on top of the suspect without any warning—a potentially dangerous situation, especially if the suspect is armed. Even on passive tracks, then, backup officers must remain vigilant and aware of their surroundings. Do not allow a dog's apparently relaxed behavior to make you complacent.

ACTIVE TRACKS

The active track is what law enforcement teams deal with the most. In an active track, the person we are following is under pressure to avoid apprehension. Usually, this is because this person has committed a crime. Whether or not they know they are being pursued, they are intent on putting as much ground between them and the crime scene as possible.

Active tracks are left by people who are under significant pressure to escape an area, such as those who have committed a crime. These suspects are under extreme stress, have elevated levels of cortisol in their system, and excrete high levels of enhanced odor. The odors emitted from a fleeing suspect, along with other odors created through ground disturbance and transference from the suspect to the surrounding environment, create a distinct scent path that is discernible to the dog, allowing the K9 team to pursue and apprehend.

As an officer attending a crime scene, you need to obtain as much intelligence as you can on the circumstances of the crime. If possible, determine how many suspects are involved, and if there are any indications that the suspect or suspects have been using drugs or drinking. Try to establish where the suspects were last seen or known to be and preserve the area—this is crucial for the K9 team. Do not allow other officers to wander into the crime scene. The fewer people that contaminate the initial crime scene, the better the opportunity for the dog to be able to determine the correct track that was left by the suspect(s). If you are attending the scene of an armed robbery, determine what type of weapon was used. If the weapon was a gun, get some idea of its caliber. If there are witnesses to the crime, obtain descriptions of the suspect or suspects, including physical descriptions and clothing. Keep in mind that many suspects discard clothing as they flee.

On the arrival of your dog team, brief your K9 handler with as much information as possible. If you are going to act as backup on an active track, obtain direction from the hander about what they expect from you both on the search and when contact is made with the suspect or suspects. The number of backup officers required will depend on circumstances. If you are a lone officer supporting the dog handler, your main function will be to go hands on and secure the suspect once they have been located. Searches for multiple suspects and potentially armed suspects will require multiple backup officers. In these cases, pull your team together for a briefing and organize who is going to perform what function when contact is made.

Considering air currents

It is important to remember that air currents can play a significant factor in K9 searches, regardless of the type of track you're following or whether you're searching for people, evidence, or contraband. There are two situations you should be particularly aware of when backing up a K9 team. The first is the possibility that the suspect is positioned above you or downwind of you (see chapter 4). This can be an extremely dangerous situation for the dog handler as the scent of the suspect is being carried on the air currents in a direction, or at a level that is not detectable by the dog.

When the scent of the suspect is being blown toward the dog, the dog will easily detect the suspect from a distance causing the dog to exhibit a more excitable behavior, indicating to the handler that the suspect is nearby. However, when the suspect is in a position where their body odor is not being carried toward the dog in the air, the dog will not recognize and indicate the suspect's scent until the team is almost on top of the suspect's location. In some cases, the suspect may have diverted off the track in such a way that the dog cannot detect the airborne scent due to the direction of air currents.

If a suspect is armed, there is potential for them to be waiting to ambush the dog team. By the time the dog realizes it has overshot the suspect's location, the handler will be well within the suspect's kill zone. In these situations, a backup team that is properly positioned and alert to its surroundings can be a deciding factor in a suspect's decision to shoot.

The second situation relates to building searches impacted by chimney effect and other indoor air current patterns (see chapter 5). These phenomena cause a strong portion of the scent to pool in a location that is a distance away from where the suspect is actually hiding. In these situations, the dog will often indicate where the buildup of scent is occurring, away from the suspect rather than near the suspect themselves. The dog is actually indicating where the strongest source of odor may be due to scent pooling resulting from air flow emanating from the suspect's location but pooling in a different location altogether. The suspect may in fact be behind you or your dog handler when the dog is indicating the scent in an area in front of you.

Given enough time, the handler will usually be able to get the dog to work to the source of the scent or be able to identify where the suspect's odor is emanating from by studying the building structure or interpreting the air flow given the environment they are in. However, this can be a dangerous situation, and it is imperative to use extreme caution when you know that air currents may be significantly affecting the search. Stay aware of your surroundings. Maintain adequate distance between you and the K9 team. Use all the caution you would if you were searching the building without the assistance of a K9 team. Always scan your surroundings and avoid focusing on what the dog is doing.

Apprehending suspects

Before you begin a search, brief with your K9 team and establish the responsibilities of everyone on the team. This briefing should include a plan for positioning of backup officers during the track and who is going to fulfil what role when taking the suspect into custody when you locate them.

Once the dog has done its job in locating the person, it is time for backup officers to step up to make the apprehension in a tactically sound manner. Should the suspect initiate a gun fight, officers who have been appropriately positioned during the track will avoid any potential crossfire situations when immediate action is taken to neutralize the threat.

A "suspect" is taken into custody after being located by a K9 team in this training exercise.

CLOSING IN ON A SUSPECT

As your K9 team closes in on a suspect, the dog will begin to give a clear indication that it is getting close. This is often referred to as a *proximity alert*. When your dog indicates that you are closing in on the suspect, shut off your flashlight if you are using one. (In general, keep in mind that, when working with a K9 team, the less you use a flashlight, the better. If you are using a flashlight, ensure you never backlight your K9 team while you are escorting them.) Ready your weapon as you move. If the dog locates a suspect, order the suspect to come out and show their hands. If at all possible, try to triangulate yourself with your K9 officer to divide the suspect's attention.

If the dog makes physical contact with the suspect, follow the direction of the K9 handler as to when to approach. When you can approach, work rapidly to control and handcuff the suspect before the handler calls the dog off. Continue to follow the handler's instructions until they call the dog off. Maintain control.

In some cases, the dog may make contact with the suspect in a location where it is not possible to go hands on in order to take the suspect into custody. An example of such circumstances would be any location with tight quarters, such as a crawl space under a home. In these situations, the handler will need to recall the dog to his/her side and direct the suspect to crawl out to open space where they can safely be taken into custody. In such cases, treat the situation the same as you would any high-risk stop: maintain cover, direct the suspect out to you, and take them into custody in your area of control.

Finally, remember that many crimes are committed by more than one suspect. Be aware of the possibility that there may be more than one suspect in close proximity to you, and be alert to the possibility of a setup or ambush. Most suspects, when fleeing together, will usually go to ground and hide within a short distance of one another.

K9 APPREHENSIONS AND LIABILITY

Working with search dogs—or any dogs, for that matter—comes with certain liabilities, particularly when they are trained in aggression. It is critical for officers to understand that the use of the dog to search for and find a suspect and the use of a dog to make a criminal apprehension are two separate applications. Deploying dogs as a use of force is a decision that comes with its own responsibilities and liabilities, and every handler has a responsibility to act ethically, use sound judgment, and uphold their department's core values when they deploy their dog.

In particular, officers need to be aware that calling in a dog as a primary use of force to make an apprehension when other methods of intervention could have been used instead is an invitation for a lawsuit. Any use of force must pass standard for objective reasonableness in court. This standard is defined in *Graham v. Connor*, 490 U.S. 386 (1989): a "reasonable" officer present at the scene would have seen the need to make the same decision. Any misuse of the dog as a use of force can result in significant repercussions not only for yourself, your fellow attending officers, the K9 handler, and your agency, but for the reputation of K9 policing as a whole.

None of this is to say that you shouldn't call in a dog team when dealing with a belligerent suspect so you can have the dog available should you need it. In fact, that would be a wise choice. The mere presence of a police dog can be a significant de-escalating factor in dangerous situations, reducing the risk of injury to both officers and suspects. Even without ever making contact with the suspect, a dog can still effectively distract a dangerous suspect, making them easier to apprehend.

Of course, there will be times when a dog is required to physically apprehend suspects. In these cases, follow the handler's lead, and stick to your plan. Any decision to use the dog for this purpose needs to be judicious, as a bad deployment is never inconsequential.[2]

2 R.S. Eden, *K9 Supervisor's Manual*, p. 100

Part II

K9 Search Skillsets

3

Tracking and Trailing

Law enforcement officers are frequently confronted with the need to locate an individual who is not present at the scene. Sometimes it is a lost person, and sometimes it is someone suspected of committing an offense. In some cases, the person would like to be found—a lost child, for instance. In other cases, the person does not want to be found and will actively work to avoid rescue or capture. For example, mentally incapacitated people, even if they have not committed a crime, are sometimes confused and think that searchers will try to hurt them. They may lay quietly in hiding and let rescuers pass within a few feet of them without revealing their location. When officers are searching for individuals suspected of crimes, those individuals may use more elaborate evasive techniques to avoid capture.

Regardless of why we are looking for someone and how they will respond to us when we make contact, a well-trained tracking or trailing dog is an invaluable tool, and can make the difference between a successful and an unsuccessful search.

A K9 team and backup on a track.

What are tracking and trailing?

We often refer to tracking and trailing dogs together. This is because both tracking and trailing dogs work in a similar manner to search for missing people and suspects who have left an identified area or crime scene. For clarity, we will give a distinct definition to these two search techniques. However, it is worth keeping in mind that in the field, you may encounter these terms being used almost interchangeably.

Though both tracking and trailing dogs make some use of ground scent (odors created when the ground is disturbed), the actual types of odors they focus on are different. For the purposes of this book, a tracking dog is a dog trained to closely follow the physical path a person has taken with their feet. This type of dog uses a combination of environmental scent types including human odor, ground disturbance, and transferred scent (odor that is transferred from once surface to another)—called the track scent—to stay as true as possible to the actual footprints of the individual it is following (figure 3).

Figure 3 Tracking dogs stay fairly close to the footprints of the missing person.

A trailing dog is trained to follow a combination of biological scent types, or body odor, that have been deposited on the ground. These odors are more likely to have been blown by the wind before they settle on the ground. Because of this, while the trailing dog is still following the person, it may not follow the person's actual footpath (figure 4).

Figure 4 Trailing dogs can be far away from the person's footprints and still be on the trail.

The unique combinations of odors that a tracking or trailing dog follows are referred to as "scent pictures." Understanding what a scent picture is will help us understand how and why the behaviors of these two types of search dogs differ.

THE SCENT PICTURE

The odors created by the passage of the human body through an area are collectively called the "scent picture." A scent picture has nothing to do with sight. Rather, just as we human beings might *look* around to get a picture of what happened at a particular scene, a dog will *smell* around to get their own "picture."

When a person walks away from a scene, they do two things. First, they disturb the environment mechanically in various ways. Second, they leave behind biological traces from their bodies. These biological traces and environmental disturbances create distinct odors that make up the scent picture. Dogs can be trained to follow the paths of these odors.

Let's begin with the environmental disturbance odors, also called the "track scent." These odors are created by the mechanical disturbance of the ground by the suspect's feet as they walk. When a person steps on vegetation or ground cover, they crush and break the outer skin of the plants or leaves, which release moisture and odors that are slightly different from and stronger than the uncrushed vegetation around them. The dog can smell these slight differences, allowing it to follow the person footprint by footprint. Even where there is no vegetation or ground cover, a track scent may be created by the weight of the person compressing the tiny particles of the soil under their feet. This compression restricts the air flow between the soil particles. This leads to a slight difference in odor between the compressed and uncompressed soils. Again, this difference is detectable by the dog and allows it to follow the person.

The other main odors that make up the scent picture are those made by the human body. They come from a person's actual epidermal (skin) cells and are referred to as "body odor." These epidermal cells (sometimes called "skin rafts") are constantly falling off of our bodies in great numbers. They fall off of us because they are, in fact, dead cells. As such, they have already begun to decompose, creating gases. The protein structure in these cells is controlled by the genetic makeup of the individual, and is therefore different from person to person; the gases created by decomposition are also different between people. It should be noted that we also breathe out cells from our lungs, leaving further trace elements of our individual odor as we move. The heavier we breathe, the more odor we leave for the dog to work with.

A significant contribution to the human "scent picture" is that odor which is created from the excretion of fluids from the apocrine glands of the human body. The apocrine system kicks in when a person is under stress, or the body is being stressed through physical exertion. Apocrine glands are found in the arms, breasts, and groin, and produce significant quantities of sweat. Fluids from the apocrine glands combine with oils from sebaceous glands and are initially odorless; however, once excreted onto the body as sweat, it combines with bacteria on the skin and quickly creates significant quantities of odor that is pungent and easily discernible. This is what we often refer to as body odor, or BO. In the context of K9 searches, we refer to it as enhanced odor.

The dog can easily discern the unique scents of these various components, decomposing skin cells and their gases, as well as other biological odors resulting from perspiration. These odors allow the dog to follow the trail quite effectively.

There are, of course, many other scents that may be relevant to a scene. These are called "secondary odors." They include, among other things, a person's aftershave or perfume, the smell of a person's shoes, their laundry or personal soap, their hairspray, their clothing material, or their diet. These can also contribute in a small way to the overall scent picture but do not hold the same relevance as a person's natural body odor.

Finally, the scent picture may include what are known as "transferred scents." These scents can be very useful to a tracking or trailing dog. A transferred scent is simply an odor that has been transferred from one surface to another. As a suspect flees across a grass surface, for example, they pick up thousands of microscopic particles on their shoes. As the suspect proceeds onto a sidewalk, these grass particles are deposited onto the paving stones. At the same time, the suspect picks up minute particles of lime and other products that make up the sidewalk. As the suspect moves onto a roadway, they continue to leave small particles from the grass surface, as well as particles from the sidewalk, and pick up small particles of tar and oil residue—and so on.

THE POINT LAST SEEN

For a tracking or trailing dog to be useful to your search, you must identify the place from which the dog's track will start. This place is called the "point last seen," or PLS. Identifying a PLS is important not only so that the dog will be able to pick up on the beginning of the track, but so that officers can connect the suspect and any evidence they find along the track to the scene.

Usually, a PLS is the last place a witness actually saw the person, but not always. It may also be the last place a person was known to have been. For instance, sometimes we know that someone jumped out of a window and fled the scene. We therefore know that even though no one saw the individual at the bottom of the window, there will be a guaranteed track somewhere outside the window. If a PLS and guaranteed source of track can be accurately identified, and if a properly trained tracking or trailing dog can be brought to the scene within a reasonable amount of time, we have a good chance of being able to trace the path the missing person used when they left the scene. This path will lead us either to the individual themselves, or to a place where their scent trail ends or weakens because, for example, they entered a building or got into a car.

TRACKING VERSUS TRAILING

The environmental and biological scents and scent transfers that make up the scent picture all leave detectable and continuous paths of odor. Regardless of whether a dog is a tracking dog or trailing dog, we call these paths the "track." Because scent pictures are very complex, there will be more than one possible way for the dog to correctly follow the track.

Here is the most important thing to understand: tracking and trailing dogs are both trained to follow a continuous stream of physical evidence left behind by the individual. In the end, both dogs will follow the track as far as it leads them—they just do it in different ways. The biggest difference between tracking and trailing dogs is the aspect of the scent picture—the type of odor—they are trained to follow. The odor type the dog follows will determine the dog's behavior. The tracking dog will largely follow the path of environmental disturbances, which aligns with a person's actual footsteps. The trailing dog will largely follow body odor, which may have drifted away from the person's footpath.

K9 Biza and Officer David Ljunggren of the Auburn Police Department (Massachusetts) work a track. © Tracy Puchalski

Both of these approaches have strengths and weaknesses. The tracking dog gives us a very good idea of where the person walked. It also brings us directly to any evidence that may have been dropped along their footpath. Relative to the trailing dog, however, the tracking dog works slowly. The trailing dog works faster, but it does not always give us a good idea of where the person actually walked. More than this, a trailing dog may fail to indicate on dropped evidence if the dog is far enough off the person's actual footpath and the wind direction carries the scent of any dropped articles downwind away from where the dog is physically trailing. In many cases, a trailing dog is using fringe odor and therefore simply not close enough to the original track left by a suspect to come across articles that the suspect has dropped along that track.

When it comes to presenting findings in court, tracking and trailing dogs can both be assets. When they are well trained, you can have confidence in the abilities of both tracking and trailing dogs' abilities to locate and follow the physical evidence they have been trained to detect. You can also have confidence in the ability of an expert witness (the dog's handler) to explain the tracking or trailing process in court when necessary. Consequently, when you need to prove that the person you found came from a particular place, such as the scene of a crime, a tracking or trailing dog is the best tool for the job. Depending on corroborative evidence, their behavior can establish a physical connection between the person you found and the place where the track or trail started; this connection will usually hold up in a court.

That being said, it is worth considering that information provided by tracking dogs, in particular, tends to be taken as stronger, more direct evidence that, in most cases, requires only slight corroboration to gain a conviction. Most courts also accept as evidence articles that were discovered by a dog on the track and that results in fingerprint or DNA recovery when the handler can articulate how their dog's track connects the recovered evidence to the crime scene.

Working with tracking and trailing dogs

There are a number of general, practical considerations to keep in mind when calling in a tracking or a trailing dog. Keeping these considerations in mind, and acting accordingly, will help the K9 teams you work with be successful.

WORKING AGAINST THE CLOCK

When you identify a situation that requires a tracking or trailing dog, call for the dog as soon as possible. Time works against tracking and trailing dogs. Once the source of the targeted odors has left the area (the person has walked away), odors begin to weaken. Environmental factors and weather begin to corrupt the scent picture: the wind disperses odors and/or the sun burns them off. As time passes, the risk of contamination by other people or vehicular movement in the area will increase. The sooner we can put a dog on a track or trail, the stronger the odors will be, and the easier it will be for the dog to follow.

PRESERVING THE SCENE

While you wait for the K9 team to arrive, you must preserve the scene! Regardless of how good the dog is at scent discrimination, all dogs find it easier to follow an uncontaminated track or trail. The key to success on most tracks is for the dog to have a clear and distinct starting point. Barring exigent circumstances, the first officer on the scene should seal off the PLS and as much space around it as possible. This officer should let no one—including detectives, administrators, firefighters, and other first responders—contaminate the area, for instance by walking all over the start of the track, until after the dog team has been deployed and is well along the track.

Depending on the dog or dogs you are working with, you may also need to preserve a scent article (something that has been touched only by the missing person and therefore smells like them). Not all dogs use scent articles to begin their trails, so ask your K9 team if they find them useful. If they do, ask them how they want you to preserve them. In most cases, such articles should be identified but not handled.

PERIMETERS AND BACKUP

When pursuing a fleeing suspect, you'll need to set up an effective perimeter around the search area. Most importantly, if there is any chance that the person you are searching for could be armed or violent, capable backup officers must be present. On high-risk deployments, it is appropriate to call in a specially trained tactical tracking team to fill this role. These officers should have trained with the K9 team so the dog is accustomed to their presence. They need to understand that the dog and handler cannot defend themselves when they are focusing on the search. It is therefore the responsibility of backup officers to provide security for the team as the track progresses. Their lives depend on a good backup team.

Even when a track or trail doesn't locate a suspect, it can succeed in other ways. A tracking or trailing application may, for example, succeed in pushing a suspect to the perimeter, where they are taken into custody by containment team members. It may also identify the missing person's direction of travel or find dropped evidence. Even losing the track or finding no track at all can provide important information: perhaps a person got into a vehicle, or perhaps they were never in an area to begin with.

4

Air Scenting and Area Searches

In some situations, officers must locate a person without the benefit of a PLS. Maybe there isn't one, or maybe there is some practical, geographical, or tactical reason not to use it. In these cases, an air-scenting dog may be the best tool for the job. This chapter will discuss air scenting as a search technique in general, and how it is applied in outdoor searches, called area searches. We will look at air scenting as an indoor search technique in chapter 5.

What is air scenting?

Many K9 teams are trained for both air scenting and tracking or trailing. Unlike tracking or trailing, which make use of ground scent, air scenting primarily uses odors present in the air: the body odor created by epithelial skin cells carried by air currents or wind and detected by the dog while they are still suspended in the air.

As we learned in chapter 2, people are constantly shedding dead skin cells. Many of these cells are carried away from the person in whatever direction the air around them happens to be moving. As the cells are carried along by the air currents, they create a cone-shaped pattern that moves away from the individual in the direction that the air is moving. The shape and nature of this cone depends on a number of factors including the speed of air currents, the weather conditions (if outdoors), the presence of environmental barriers, and the movement of the person.

The influence of air current and the surrounding environment on air scenting is not insignificant. They can cause the cone to have an irregular shape and, in some cases, cause gaps in the scent cone, called dead zones. It is imperative that officers working with air-scenting dogs have a basic understanding of air currents, how they interact with the surrounding environment, and ultimately how they influence the odor that the dog is following. Without this understanding, air currents can cause complications and officers can misinterpret a dog's behavior.

What is an area search?

Area searching is an application of air-scenting search techniques in large, outdoor spaces. In an area search, the dog will try to locate the scent cone and work toward its point of origin. If it is safe and practical to do so, the K9 handler will take the area-search dog to the downwind side of the search area and begin a grid search into the wind. The idea is to present the dog with every possible air sample in the search area. Since this process is one of the handler's main responsibilities, you should expect them to be very particular about their search pattern and to fight against anything (including you, if necessary) that may disrupt it.

At some point, the concentration of skin cells carried by the wind becomes strong enough for the dog to recognize. At this point, the dog will leave the handler and run laterally to the wind until it leaves the scent cone. When it runs out of odor because it has left the scent cone, the dog will reverse direction, running back into the cone and continue until it leaves the cone again on the other side, at which point it will reverse direction again. This is often referred to as "bracketing the odor." After a few lateral moves, the dog will determine the basic shape of the scent cone and quickly run up the cone into the air current or wind toward the area with the strongest odor at the tip—toward, that is, your target individual (figure 5).

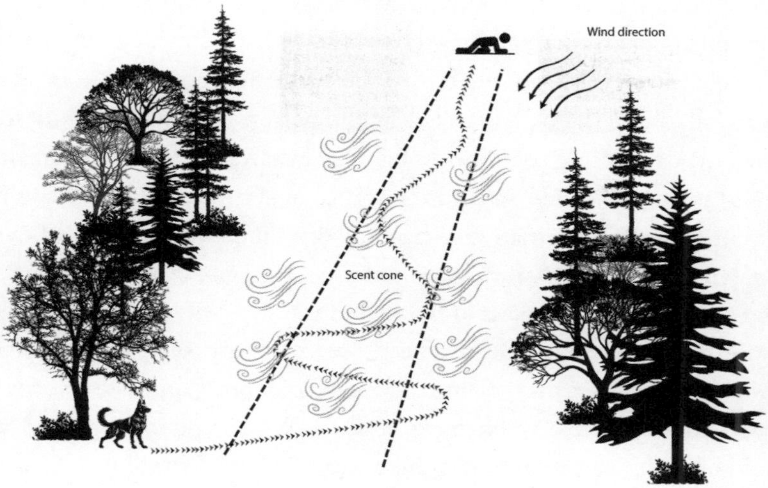

Figure 5 The dog is deployed off-line to search freely in an area-search deployment. As the dog casts out and encounters wind-borne scent, it will vector back and forth, in and out of the scent cone, until it finds the strongest scent, ultimately following it to its source.

ADVANTAGES OF AREA SEARCHES

Like other dogs, area-search dogs are able to search large areas much more quickly and accurately than human searchers. Unlike tracking and trailing dogs, however, area-search dogs do not need a PLS or a scent article in order to begin or be effective in their search. This can be a huge advantage when you have a large area to search, and especially when you have been unable to identify a specific point from which to begin the search.

What's more, the process of air scenting works well even if the person you are looking for moves locations, so long as they remain within a defined search area. The dog knows that it must find the strongest source of odor, and that source will typically be the person. As the person moves, their scent cone moves. A dog using air-scenting techniques will be able to immediately react to this movement, and continue approaching the scent cone's source.

This search strategy is quite different from tracking or trailing. In tracking and trailing, dogs follow a more or less meandering path largely dictated by the odors they are detecting on or close to the ground, along the path traveled by the person the team is trying to locate. Air scenting could be thought of, instead, as traveling more or less "as the crow flies" toward the source of the odor. This makes air scenting a good alternative to tracking or trailing in situations where the person has been moving around the same general area for hours, creating a confusing mess of tracks and trails.

Area-search dogs have also been used to find people in situations where no track exists—for instance, people trapped under deep snow after an avalanche or submerged in water. While a person's track may end or be covered in these circumstances, human odor will float to the surface of snow or water, and an air-scenting dog may still be able to find them.

DISADVANTAGES OF AREA SEARCHES

Of course, area searches also have their weaknesses. One important weakness to consider when using an air-scenting dog is that you will not be able to prove in court where a person came from using the information the dog gives you. You will also not be able to explain to the courts exactly where the person walked. This is a consequence of one of the dog's strengths: because it doesn't use a PLS, it does not follow the person from any specific starting point.

Area-search dogs, like other dogs, may also recover dropped evidence. Note, however, that in an area-search context, this evidence cannot be clearly connected to the crime involved without further, corroborative evidence, as there is no distinct track from the scene or to the suspect that can connect the recovered evidence to that individual.

AIR CURRENTS AND DEAD ZONES IN AREA SEARCHES

Air currents in outdoor search areas can cause challenges for area-search dogs. Let's consider an example. Say we are conducting an area search, and the wind in the area is strong. Though we don't know it yet, the person we are looking for is hiding high in a tree.

Because of their position, the person's odor is carried high on the wind for a certain distance before dropping to a level where the dog can detect it.

If the handler starts the dog on the downwind side of the search area, the dog will find the scent cone at a point where it is close enough to the ground to be detected and will begin work the scent cone normally. Eventually, the dog will reach a dead zone—an area in which the odor a dog is following suddenly disappears (figure 6). This loss of odor is due to the thermal dynamics created by the tree. The interior of

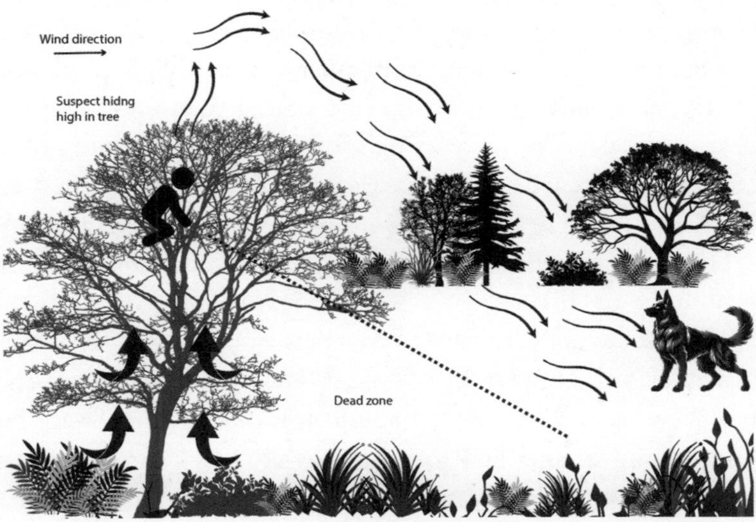

Figure 6 Side view of a suspect hiding high in a tree. The tree's interior is warmer than its exterior and naturally draws in cool air at its base that is then expelled near the top of the tree as it warms. The suspect's body heat also warms the air around them, causing it to rise along with their body odor. Odor rises out of the tree and then drifts in the direction of the wind, gradually falling as it cools.

In most cases, this phenomenon will create a dead zone near the base of the tree where there is no odor for a search dog to detect. The dog will, instead, detect the odor where it exists: away from the base of the tree, where it falls back to ground-level. When a search dog indicates on an odor, it is the handler's responsibility to interpret the behavior and the circumstances of the search to determine the location of the person.

the tree, especially with the body heat of a person, causes odor to rise up the trunk of the tree because the air under the tree is cooler than the air around the trunk. In effect, this causes the suspects scent to rise instead of falling. As the scent rises, it will normally exit the branches of the trees above where the suspect is hiding and follow the path of the prevailing wind or breeze. The odor can travel some distance before it drops back to the ground, where it will again be detectable by the dog. In the dead zone, the dog will behave as though it has lost the odor (which it has) and is unable to find the person (which it can't). This is where K9 handlers must understand and recognize odor loss indications by their dogs and why it is paramount that backup officers who escort the K9 teams be aware of their surroundings.

Air currents can wreak havoc in other ways as well. For instance, if a K9 team ends up on the upwind side of the suspect they are looking for, the dog may pass right by the suspect without giving a proximity alert. This is because the wind is coming in a direction that causes the scent to drift away from the dog rather than toward it. Despite its proximity to the suspect, the dog does not detect the scent in the air currents.

Dead zones are particularly dangerous situations for K9 teams, as they give the suspect an advantage over incoming officers and may allow them to set up an ambush. It is therefore important for officers to understand how to recognize this type of situation when they encounter it. If officers do not understand air currents, they may think the dog has failed when it lost the scent. They may even lose confidence in the abilities of their dog teams to locate people. However, if the officers understand air currents and take them into consideration, they will see that the dog has not failed at all. It has, in fact, done exactly what it has been trained to do.

Remember that a search dog's job is to provide us with raw information. It is our job to interpret this information. An experienced dog handler would interpret the dog's behavior as follows. The dog's scent-following behavior leading up to the dead zone tells the handler that the person is present, and is somewhere in the direction in which the dog was last giving positive indications. When the dog suddenly loses the air scent, the handler knows that there is a strong possibility that the person is in a location that is preventing the dog from detecting the odor.

Far from failing, then, the dog's behavior combined with the handler's expert interpretation has given us at least three pieces of crucial information about this situation. First, we know that there is definitely a person in the search area. Second, we know that the person is upwind of the place where the dog started working the scent cone. Third, we know that the person is possibly up high or in a location where the environment is preventing the dog from detecting the odor. This is a great deal more information than we had before we deployed the dog. All of this information can help to further the search by narrowing down the search area and having assisting officers look for the suspect in high places.

Working with area-search dogs

As with other searches, there are a few general considerations to keep in mind when working with area-search dogs.

PERIMETERS AND BACKUP

When doing an area search, it is usually best to clear the search area of bystanders—for instance, by confining residents to the interior of their homes while the search is in progress—so that the only person in the search area other than involved officers and search teams is the person they are actively looking for. This allows the dog team to zero in on the intended target individual, and only that person.

If a missing person wants to be found, or at least is not trying to evade the K9 team, it is not necessary to create a perimeter around the search area. However, if the person is trying to evade you, a perimeter should be set up as soon as possible to contain the suspect—hopefully before the K9 team arrives. This includes air unit support if it is available.

It is also important to remember that, like other search dogs, air-scenting dogs and their handlers cannot focus properly on the search and look out for themselves at the same time. You must provide for their safety. This is, perhaps, especially true in situations involving dead zones. Given enough time, the dog and K9 handler are likely to find the scent and, eventually, the suspect. Until then, however, they will need good backup so they can focus on their work.

TIME IS ON YOUR SIDE

Once the search area is cleared and the perimeter, if needed, is in place, time is on our side. As long as the person remains in the search area, you do not need to rush to get the dog into action. This larger time window differs significantly from the use of tracking and trailing techniques, which use odors that weaken and risk contamination as time passes. For air-scenting dogs, as long as the person remains in the search area, their odors will remain strong.

As in other searches, having an extra few moments to prepare an air search dog for action can be hugely beneficial to the search.

LOCATING THE PERSON OR SUSPECT

The nature of an area search can differ depending on what the dog is trained to do when it locates the targeted individual. Many utility dogs are trained primarily for criminal searches and are expected to immediately bite anyone they find in the search area. Other agencies expect their dogs to sit and bark unless the person tries to escape, at which point they bite and hold them to prevent the escape. Some agencies search with dogs that have no aggression training and either sit and bark to indicate that they have located a person or do what is known as a "re-find" where the dog returns to the handler and gives a specific signal to indicate it has located the person, at which point the handler leaves the search pattern and follows the dog to the person.

These different approaches each have different legal consequences which are contested in court, and legal opinions can change over time in accordance with case law. What remains constant is that officers need to follow departmental policy and procedure when they deploy search dogs. Make certain that your department has a policy for deploying dogs and that you operate within them at all times.

For example, at the present time, many agencies do not authorize the deployment of dogs with aggression training unless the person being sought is suspected of committing a violent felony. If the person is suspected of committing a misdemeanor, aggression-trained dogs are not deployed to find them. This may change with time and varies agency to agency, so always check department policy, and make sure you are in compliance with it.

5

Building Searches

Police officers are frequently expected to determine if a building is empty or if there is someone inside, such as when they attend the scene of burglary or a burglar alarm where a door is found to be insecure. While police officers can do this work on their own, it is done much more quickly and accurately with a dog. More than this, using search dogs to clear buildings saves personnel hours and allows officers to spend more time on patrol and responding to other calls.[3]

A K9 team can be a valuable addition to building entries and searches.

3 See the discussion of the Lansing study on the efficiency of police dogs in Eden, *K9 Supervisor's Manual*, 4–8.

What is a building search?

Dogs that are capable of tracking on hard top (e.g., concrete) are capable of tracking people inside a building from a point of entry. It is often more efficient and tactically sound, however, to conduct an indoor air-scenting search, referred to as a *building search*.

As we know from chapter 4, air-scenting dogs follow the airborne skin cells and odors being produced and shed by the body of the missing person or suspect to their source. In fact, a building search is simply an area search with well-defined borders and, often, unique air currents.

Unique air flow aside, the dog still gives you the significant advantage of being able to search large structures much faster and more accurately than human officers. The fact that dogs can find things we cannot see is particularly useful in building searches, allowing us to search a room or closet without having to open the door or touch a light switch. This is a distinct advantage when dealing with dangerous individuals.

AIR CURRENTS AND DEAD ZONES IN BUILDING SEARCHES

When working with dogs in building search contexts, officers will do well to remember two things. First, search dogs indicate the point at which they find the strongest target odor, not necessarily the source of the odor (in this case, the person you are looking for). This first point is explained by the second: the dynamics of air currents within buildings can be unexpectedly complicated. In fact, air currents are especially unreliable in buildings, and may cause more complications inside than they do outside.

As in other area searches, dogs will "bracket the odor," or scent cone, when they find it. The scent is weakest at the edges of the cone and strongest at the center. As the dog moves from edge to edge, the officer can estimate the approximate location of the suspect by determining the center point of the outer brackets indicated by the dog. In a building with minimal airflow, the scent of someone hiding high, for example, will fall and dissipate in a cone-like pattern (figure 7). The dog will bracket the scent on each side and gradually work to where the scent is strongest—usually directly below where the suspect is hiding.

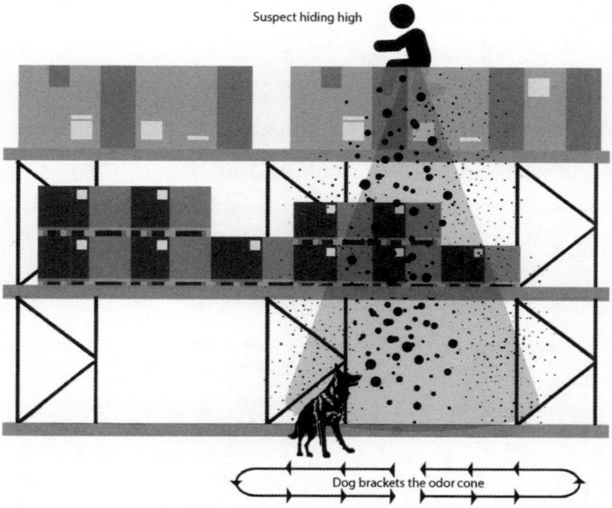

Figure 7 A K9 brackets the scent cone of a suspect hiding up high in a building with minimal airflow.

Things change when we introduce more complicated air currents. Let's say a person is hiding near a place where air is exiting the building—perhaps they are next to an air vent that is sucking air out of the room to circulate it. In this case, the person's odor is being pushed out of the building rather than circulating through it. There would be very little odor available inside the building for the dog to detect. The dog would therefore need to come very close to where the suspect is hiding in order to see the suspect visually or smell them. These places are typically few in number, but they do need to be identified and searched visually by officers.

Air vents are, however, not the only ways that buildings can produce complex air currents. Let's look at another scenario. You are conducting a building search with an air-scenting dog. Unbeknownst to you, the person you are looking for is hiding against the warmest wall in the building (in the northern hemisphere, this is usually the south-facing wall). All of a sudden, the dog performs its final response behavior. The dog has not found the person you are looking for; instead, it is facing the completely bare north wall of the building.

In this case, you are likely witnessing the "chimney effect" at work (figure 8). The chimney effect (sometimes called the "up and over" effect) refers to a passive movement of warm and cool air. As air gets warmer, it rises and is replaced with cooler air. When this effect takes place in a confined area such as a building, the air begins to flow in a circular pattern: the air rises against one wall as it warms, flows across the ceiling, falls against the opposite wall as it cools, and is pushed by the air behind it back to where it began.

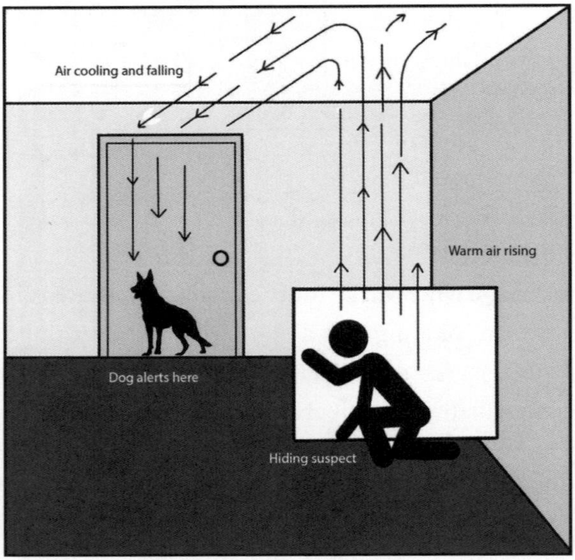

Figure 8 The chimney effect in action.

The chimney effect very neatly explains our scenario above: because the person is hiding against the warmest wall of a building, their odor is carried up with the warm air currents and begins to circulate within the room. When the odor is flowing along the ceiling, it is too high up for the dog to detect. It is only when it comes down on the opposite wall that the dog is able to detect it. However, as the dog cannot fly, it cannot follow the odor to its source. Although the dog may be standing in front of a completely blank wall, it has nonetheless found the best and strongest source of human odor in the building—so it performs its final response behavior. The dog is not in error; it has actually done its job well. It has given us more information than we had before. It is up to the handler to interpret the dog's behavior and subsequently try to locate the source of odor.

While the dog in this scenario is not in front of the person we are looking for, it has behaved in ways that, if we understand the dynamics of air flow within buildings and can interpret the behaviors correctly, will give us a great deal of information. First, if the perimeter is intact, the officers now know that there is definitely someone in the building. Second, they know the odor is coming from up high, where the dog cannot follow it. Third, they know that the person is likely hiding against or near the warmest wall of the building, because their scent is being taken up in a warm air current. If the officers can figure out where the warm air is coming from, they may find the person.

These are only two examples of how air flow complicates searches. As an officer on a K9 building search, keep an open mind and be a detective when dogs indicate odor in strange places, or when they don't indicate at all. Always ask yourself where that air is coming from, or where it is going. If you can understand how the air is flowing, you may well find your suspect.

Perimeters and backup

In a building search, the person is typically a suspect trying to evade capture. This being the case, the first step to a successful building search is the same as the first step to any search within a defined area: establish a perimeter.

Secondly, stay alert. Be aware of your surroundings and potential danger points. Don't focus on the dog, focus on places of potential ambush. This is, of course, something to keep in mind in all K9 searches. However, because of the odd nature of air currents in buildings, building searches pose a particular danger. For some reason, many officers feel that once the dog takes over, they no longer have to be concerned with normal precautions. Do not throw out all your training and experience simply because a dog is working. Use good tactics to clear the building, and provide effective backup for your K9 team.

Because a building search involves air scenting, once the perimeter is up around the building, time is on your side. Because the source of odor (the person) is confined to the search area, the odor will remain strong, getting stronger with time, and will therefore provide good search conditions for the dog.

6

Detection

To this point in the book, we have focused on dogs trained to find living people. Detector dogs are dogs trained to search for and locate substances, helping human searchers find things that might otherwise be imperceptible to them. They have been proved to be effective in a wide range of profiles, from narcotics and explosives to human remains and illicit produce at border points. There are even hotel security dog teams trained to detect bed bug infestations and gas leak detection dogs trained to scan for gas leaks from buried pipelines. There really is no limit to the capabilities and variety of solutions well-trained detector dogs can provide.

The purpose of detector dogs in a law enforcement context is to recognize and locate target odors to allow law enforcement to take the next necessary steps in an investigation. For our purposes in this chapter, we will discuss five profiles that are especially relevant to law enforcement: narcotics, explosives, accelerants, human remains, and wildlife.

Detector dogs are especially useful in law enforcement because they are minimally intrusive. Using their olfactory capabilities, a detector dog can quickly scan a specific item or area that officers are either physically unable or otherwise not legally permitted to search to determine if a targeted odor is present. They are further able to do this without disturbing a scene or opening an object that may contain a target odor. Well-trained detector dogs provide relatively inexpensive, safe, and accurate detection of materials of interest to law enforcement.

Regardless of the type of detector dog you are working with, the manner of deployments and how you work in coordination with them are basically the same. Preserve the scene until the team arrives to prevent any contamination, and assist the handler as directed.

Single- and dual-purpose dogs in detection

It is important to note that detector dogs are only trained in one detection profile, that is, one category of odor. For example, a dog trained for narcotics detection will not be trained for explosives detection. The reason for this is simple: training a dog on different profiles would be dangerous. If such a dog were to indicate the presence of a target odor, the handler would be unable to know what type of odor the dog was detecting, and it would be impossible to know how to safely search the area. There's a big difference, after all, in responding to the presence of narcotics versus explosives.

This does not mean, however, that detector dogs are trained on only one odor. Rather, they are trained on a range of odors within their profile. The dog's detection profile and the place and time in which it is working will determine which and how many odors the dog is trained to recognize. Narcotics detection dogs might, for example, be trained on six to eight different narcotics odors. Explosives detection dogs, meanwhile, are typically trained on many more odors, which are chosen according to the most common and current threats in the area of the world where they will be working. Dogs in some agencies may be trained and required to accurately recognize and locate more than thirty different explosives odors.

It is also important to note that dogs trained on a detection profile may be single purpose (trained only for detection) or dual purpose (trained for detection and as a patrol dog). Some agencies will only deploy single-purpose detector dogs as they don't want the potential liability that comes with deploying a patrol dog for suspect apprehensions. Agencies that have specific mandates, such as units that focus on drug enforcement, explosives teams, or arson investigation teams with dogs trained for accelerant detection, will normally deploy only single-purpose detector dogs.

Many dogs can, however, be trained to perform both detection and patrol duties very effectively. In Canada, most police dogs are trained to perform all the functions of a patrol dog and are cross-trained on a detection profile.

Preserving and securing a search area

Different K9 units have different preferences about how you should preserve search areas for them. Find out what the preferences of your local units are and provide them with properly preserved search areas.

In narcotics searches involving vehicles, for instance, the most important action you can take when preparing for a K9 team to scan the vehicle is to simply ensure the vehicle is protected from the dangers of nearby traffic so the team can work safely. In human remains contexts, since the source of odor will not move, a perimeter is usually not necessary for a detector dog to be successful.

When the substance in question is explosives, preserving the search area for the K9 team involves sealing off a wide area and removing everyone to a safe distance without touching or moving anything as you leave. Do not turn any electrical systems on or off, open any doors, or move anything. Even turning on a light could activate a device and cause an explosion. Ensure you are complying with any written departmental protocols regarding these situations.

When a dog does find a target odor, the location is often a crime scene and should be treated as such. The area should be properly taped off and access limited for forensics specialists. Any items discovered at the scene should be treated as evidence to be used in a courtroom setting, complete with a chain of evidence being maintained by sworn law enforcement officers.

Alerts in detection

To accomplish their task, detector dogs are trained to perform a specific, trained final response when they detect a target odor. Final responses help dog handlers determine both that an odor is present and where to search further for the source of the odor.

Recall that three conditions must be satisfied for a dog's behavior to be considered a final response: it must change its behavior as it begins to work the odor; it must exhibit its trained final response when it thinks it has done enough to be rewarded; and the handler must be satisfied that the dog's behavior indicates that it has completed its job. Also remember that, at the end of the day, the handler's interpretation of the dog's behavior is the most important factor in whether or not an alert is called.

PASSIVE AND ACTIVE FINAL RESPONSES

The manner in which a detector dog signals to its handler that it has found something will vary. Some dogs are trained to dig out objects of interest themselves. This type of behavior is commonly referred to as an "active," "positive," or "aggressive" final response. Dogs trained in this type of final response scratch or bite to get at the source of the odor they are following. Other detector dogs are trained to sit or lie down and stare intently at an area of interest to signal that they have found something. This is commonly known as a "passive" final response.

K9 Jorah indicating on a hand gun. © Melinda Ruopp

Dogs trained to perform a passive final response offer two significant advantages over those trained in active final responses. First, they are much less likely to get hurt, especially if the object or substance they are looking for is explosive or poisonous, or if the area is boobytrapped. Active-response dogs have been killed through the inadvertent ingestion of poisons or narcotics during a search. Passive-response dogs are far less vulnerable to these types of dangers.

Second, passive-response dogs are able to search any target without causing major damage to property or evidence. This is not true of an active-response dog. A detector dog scratching the interior of a high-end vehicle, for example, can cause significant damage very quickly. If law enforcement ultimately finds nothing in the vehicle, the agency may end up being responsible for subsequent repairs.

K9 Biza searches a car for contraband without causing damage.
© Tracy Puchalski

ALERTS WITHOUT FINAL RESPONSE BEHAVIORS

Officers must understand and accept that handlers may sometimes call alerts even when the dog does not exhibit its specific trained final response behavior—normally, the second requirement of an alert.

A well-trained dog will usually give a final response when it detects the specific location of a target odor. In some cases, however, and depending on a number of environmental and circumstantial factors, a dog may detect an odor but not, or not immediately, perform its trained final response behavior. For instance, a narcotics detection dog may become overwhelmed by the strength of the odor given off by very large amounts of narcotics—say, an entire tractor-trailer load. Never having encountered such a large amount in training, the dog may become confused about whether or not it should complete its final response behavior since it has never been rewarded for responding to this specific stimulus.

Officers must understand that it is not necessary for the dog to perform a final response for the handler to know that the dog has detected a target odor in the area. The handler knows the dog very well and will be able to understand subtle changes in the dog's behavior that are indicative of a target odor in the search area.

When a dog senses a target odor, it will by its very nature show a change of behavior that is easily recognizable to the handler. Often, the dog will become more excited, its breathing may quicken, and it will begin to search more intensely as it senses it is closing in to the target source. Sometimes, there is so much odor in a confined area that the dog will not perform a final response at all. Still, the handler will know by the changes in their dog's behavior that target odor is present and in very close proximity.

In situations like the narcotics example above, an experienced handler would notice that their dog has worked a target odor close to the source. Even if the dog does not show its trained final response, the handler may decide that the significant change of behavior nonetheless warrants them calling an alert. If a handler calls such an alert and can articulate why based on their training and experience, their expertise should be respected. When it comes to calling alerts, everything rests on the handlers.

Detection profiles

Contraband narcotics and detection of improvised explosive devices, or IEDs, are the most common uses of detector dogs in law enforcement. Dogs trained to detect accelerants, human remains, and wildlife are also useful tools in specific types of investigations—for example, arson cases, missing persons, and poaching. The following sections go over these profiles one by one, highlighting aspects of searches that are specific to each profile and relevant to patrol officers.

NARCOTICS DETECTION DOGS

Searching for narcotics is often complicated by having to deal with large or difficult areas, large numbers of items (luggage or packages) or vehicles, and legal restrictions. Narcotics detection dogs are able to search large areas and large numbers of items much faster and more efficiently, and often less invasively, than humans.

If you need to search for narcotics in an area that is for some reason difficult to search, or if you need to obtain legal permission to conduct a narcotics search in the first place, a dog trained in narcotics detection can be a great help. For example, a narcotics detection dog can work around the exterior of a vehicle or scan packages on a conveyor belt to determine if the odor of narcotics is present without opening either the car or the packages. In both cases, a warrant for a physical search could be issued on the basis of a dog's indication of the presence of contraband.

Officer Shelby Wright and K9 Loki of the Lakewood Police Department (Colorado) search the exterior of a vehicle for narcotics odor. © Kristen Miller

SPECIAL FACTORS IN NARCOTICS DETECTION

Most times, the odor of the narcotics will lead the dog directly to its target, but not always. Their search may be complicated by several factors.

Some suspects, for example, try to use non-narcotic substances such as coffee or air fresheners to mask the odor of the narcotics. When dogs are well trained, however, these masking odors will be ineffective.

More difficult for narcotics detection dogs are narcotics that have been kept in a certain location for a long time, then removed just before the dog begins searching. Although the substance is gone, the odor remains for a time. Dogs are accustomed to responding to things they cannot see and may indicate this residual odor.

Officers should also be alert to the possible complications of air current. Be ready to compensate for the fact that dogs respond to the odor, not the source. For instance, consider a situation in which you have just stopped a vehicle that had narcotics hidden in the front engine compartment. In this situation, the dog may perform a response behavior at the rear of the vehicle. This is because, in this freshly stopped vehicle, the forward movement of the car and the air flow from the front to the back of the vehicle may cause the odor to pool in pockets near the rear bumper. The rear bumper is, therefore, where the dog can readily detect the odor. When searching this vehicle pursuant to an indication by the dog, if you do not find the source of the odor near where the dog has indicated, expand your search. Keep in mind external factors that might affect airflow and search accordingly.

You also need to be aware of air flow dynamics when searching for narcotics in buildings. If the narcotics are hidden next to an air vent drawing air out of a room for circulation, the air around the source may not move in the dog's direction. If that's the case, the dog will not be able to detect the odor or may indicate instead where that air current is exiting. Once the dog has indicated and an alert has been called, it is up to officers to find the air current's path and source.

As in building searches for human targets, these areas need to be identified and searched. K9 handlers are experts in airflow dynamics and will be able to guide assisting officers as to the best places to search (see chapter 4).

To the uninformed, the dog may seem to be wrong when it indicates far from the physical location of a target substance or does not indicate at all. Know that it is not. The dog has provided us with information (which is its primary job), namely, that the odor of narcotics is or is not present in the location it is searching. In the scenario in which narcotics were removed from the search location before the dog was deployed, the dog is correctly telling us that narcotics were present recently, even if they are not present now. In the scenarios with the recently stopped car and the exiting air current, the dog is correctly indicating that narcotics are present in the search location, even if they aren't exactly where the dog indicated. In the scenario involving the air vent and no indication from the dog, the dog is correctly telling us that it cannot smell any narcotics in that specific spot, even if narcotics are present somewhere in the location being searched. Officers and handlers must use the information the dog gives them and decide how best to proceed.

NARCOTICS DETECTION DOGS AND THE LAW

At present, most countries' laws indicate that the air around an object is not private property and therefore allow search dogs to sample it by sniffing. While the laws may change, for the moment, if a dog trained in the detection of narcotic odors indicates odor in the air around an object, many countries consider this to be probable cause for either a search or a search warrant. Be sure to know the applicable laws in your jurisdiction.

What is acceptable in the deployment of narcotics detection dogs varies according to law, most importantly case law. Since new cases are frequently decided, it is important to keep abreast of them and to make certain your departmental protocols reflect the latest developments.

A case of note for officers working with narcotics detection dogs is *Rodriguez v. United States*, 575 U.S. 348 (2015). In this case, the US Supreme Court decided that the length of time for a traffic stop may not be extended to conduct a dog sniff, as the use of the dog to sniff for drugs is unrelated to the original purpose of the stop. If you intend on calling in a dog to search for narcotics, you must have other reasons to extend the length of a stop. If, however, a dog is close by and can be deployed during the normal time frame of the traffic stop, the use of the dog is permitted.

EXPLOSIVES DETECTION DOGS

Due to instances of ongoing domestic and foreign terrorism, the need for dogs trained to detect the odors of explosive materials and devices has grown significantly. As in other types of detection work, dog-led searches for explosives are accurate and efficient, and can cover large areas. Explosives detection dogs can be trained to detect the odor of every major type of explosive material, making these searches comprehensive. And of course, dogs can find things we cannot see, and they can complete searches without having to open doors, turn on light switches in the dark, or move anything in the search area. This is a major advantage when you are trying not to activate triggers on explosive devices.

An officer and K9 search a customs vehicle for explosives in Brazil.

SPECIAL FACTORS IN EXPLOSIVES DETECTION

Explosives odors travel differently on air currents than other odors. Being somewhat heavier than narcotic odors, they tend to sink more and may create a different dispersal pattern. This can influence the way in which handlers of explosives detection dogs approach their search patterns compared to other detection profiles. As a patrol officer, it's important to be aware that these differences exist, and know that the handler is doing their job.

Another difference between explosives searches and other searches is what happens after an alert has been called. When the K9 team calls an alert in a scenario involving possible explosives, their job is done. Even if they have not identified the exact location of the odor's source (for instance, if air currents have had a significant impact on where the dog indicates the odor), it is not their job to search any further. It is no longer a K9 call. It is time for the area to be secured from a distance and for the scene to be turned over to explosive ordinance disposal (EOD) technicians specially trained in handling explosives. Continuing to search after an alert has been called would add unnecessary risk.

Remember that the most important information in these situations is whether or not explosives odors are present. Understanding air currents may allow you to identify and communicate the approximate location of the explosives to the EOD technicians after an alert has been called. As in narcotics searches, however, in cases where the explosive device or materials may have been moved just prior to the search, there may still be enough residual odor to cause the dog to respond. For example, an explosives dog may indicate on the trunk of a vehicle, but a subsequent investigation by EOD technicians shows there is no explosive material in the vehicle. Still, the dog has provided useful information: it has told you that explosives *have* been in the vehicle recently. In this case, the vehicle may have been used to transport a quantity of explosives which were removed before it came under law enforcement scrutiny.

ACCELERANT DETECTION DOGS

Fire investigators are always interested in how a fire started. Among other things, knowing the source of a fire can help investigators determine whether an arson has been committed.

If investigators suspect that the fire was deliberately started with the use of an accelerant such as gasoline or kerosene, they need to have their suspicions confirmed by a laboratory. This involves collecting samples from the scene and sending them to the lab for analysis. The challenge for investigators is to decide from where in a large, charred, burned-out structure they should take the samples. A dog trained to detect the odors of accelerants can be a big help in these situations.

Accelerant detection dogs are predominately single-purpose dogs trained to detect accelerant odors only, and not as patrol dogs. In fact, accelerant detection dogs are trained and handled by fire departments and will not be assigned to a law enforcement agency. These dogs can detect the odors of accelerants even after a fire. At a scene where visual cues are almost useless—such as a fire scene where everything is black and charred—accelerant detection dogs still search well and are usually able to indicate the best location for investigators to collect samples.

When working in buildings that have been structurally compromised, dogs present another advantage: they are lighter in weight than a human being, let alone a group of humans. They therefore do not place as much physical stress on damaged structures and reduce the risk of structural collapse. Dogs search well without having to move objects or parts of the already damaged and possibly unsafe structure. On top of this, many accelerant detection dogs are trained to give passive final responses so as to not disturb something which might be an important support in a damaged structure.

HUMAN REMAINS DETECTION DOGS

Much of this book has dealt with how search dogs can help officers who are looking for missing persons and fleeing suspects—people who are, or are presumed to be, alive. Sometimes, however, officers are searching for someone who is presumed, known, or turns out to be dead. In these cases, human remains detection (HRD) dogs, sometimes referred to as cadaver dogs, are a great help.

Trained HRD dogs can detect the odor of human remains in the air and follow it to the source. They can also detect the odor of human remains when it is seeping through the ground or snow from a buried body, or through water when the remains are submerged.

CORRECTING A MISCONCEPTION

Some people believe that any dog, whether or not it is trained in HRD, will respond to or show an interest in dead human tissue, particularly if they have been trained to detect and follow live human odors. This is a misconception that must be corrected in order to fully appreciate the value of specially trained HRD dogs.

The odor of dead humans is quite different from that of the living. It is so different that when a person walks away from a scene and then dies, some good tracking and trailing dogs will follow the track well until they encounter the pooled odor of the dead body, then lose the track. Some dogs will even become extremely disturbed, raise their hackles, go into avoidance behaviors, and refuse to search any further. Detector dogs trained on other odor profiles may simply ignore the odor of human remains and keep searching.

To understand these behaviors, remember the cardinal rule of scent detection: you should never expect a dog to do something it has not been specifically trained to do. If a dog has never been rewarded for indicating the odor of human remains in training, it will ignore this odor or give an atypical response.

When dogs not conditioned specifically to detect human remains do show an interest in human remains, the response is often unreliable. Some will show an interest in the remains of game animals as often as they will show an interest in the remains of a human being. Dogs occasionally do unusual things that end up helping us, but such instances are happy accidents. To be confident that you are getting reliable information from your search dogs, it is important to select a dog that is specifically trained to detect what you're looking for. So, when you suspect the missing person may be deceased, you should call for an HRD dog.

Law enforcement agencies will not normally have an assigned HRD dog. If you need to call in an HRD dog, you will likely need to contact a local search-and-rescue team. Often, these teams are organized through civilian support groups.

SPECIAL FACTORS IN HRD

Air currents have been discussed in other chapters, but we haven't yet seen the issues that water can add to the mix. In HRD in particular, rain can be a complication. Hard rain can temporarily wash the odor of buried remains further down into the soil so it does not reach the dog. For this reason, it is often smarter to search for buried remains when it is not raining.

It is also not unusual for the odor of human remains to be pulled deep by currents in a river only to rise to the surface farther downstream. The dog will only be able to detect and indicate the odor when it comes to the surface. In such a situation, of course, we will not find the human remains directly under the area where the dog indicated. Still, the dog has in fact it has found the best and strongest human odor available, and has correctly indicated this to us. Even in this difficult situation, the dog has provided us with much more information than we had before it went to work. First, the dog has confirmed that there are definitely human remains in the water. Second, the odor is coming from deep water where the dog could not follow it. Finally, the human remains will be found upstream from the place where the dog indicated. Just as with air currents, if we can understand the dynamics of the water currents, we will find the human remains.

In shallow water, odor and skin rafts can often float to the surface and travel downstream on top of the water. This can offer the dog an opportunity to follow the scent closer to the source.

With human remains, unlike with searches for living subjects, since the source of the odor will not move, time is not a critical factor for the dog's searching abilities. In the case of buried bodies in particular, present opinion is that chemicals in the bodies change the chemistry of the soil and give it a different odor from the soil around it. Dogs are able to detect this odor difference for a long time and have been known to indicate gravesites that are many years old.

WILDLIFE DETECTION DOGS

Enforcing game laws is just as demanding as any other type of law enforcement—indeed, sometimes more so. Many people do not realize, for instance, that bile from the gall bladder of a black bear can command a higher price on the street than heroin, and that ground-up antlers are extremely valuable on the black market. With this kind of profit motive, poachers and smugglers can be just as dangerous and devious as any other type of criminal.

In cases of suspected wildlife poaching and smuggling, officers are often confronted with the need to search large outdoor areas, vehicles, buildings, and coolers for which suspicion alone does not provide probable cause. In these cases, dogs trained to find the odors of dead wildlife can be a great help.

SPECIAL FACTORS IN WILDLIFE DETECTION

It is true that dogs without specific training in wildlife detection may show an interest in game meat. However, this natural interest is not a replacement for specific training. As with HRD dogs, dogs that aren't trained in wildlife detection will not provide us with reliable or specific information. For instance, they are just as likely to indicate the odors of unprotected species as protected ones. Wildlife detection dogs are trained on specific wildlife odors and give passive final responses when they find their target in order to avoid damaging evidence. When working in the context of game laws, then, it is better to rely on dogs that are specially trained in this field, and to know exactly which species these dogs are trained to detect.

Some wildlife officers prefer to work with dual-purpose dogs that are trained in wildlife detection and as patrol dogs. Such dogs provide a degree of handler protection—something that is especially important for wildlife officers, as they often work alone, their nearest backup may be more than a half hour away, and nearly everyone they meet is armed with edged weapons, firearms, or both. In cases of poaching, a dual-purpose dog's article search skills can be helpful in locating cartridge casings and other evidence that can support our case. In many cases, wildlife officers will also find themselves using their dogs to track potential suspects. Wildlife detection dogs have even been known to follow the trail of dragged carcasses from the scene of a poaching to the suspect's home.

Think dog!

The canine species is a unique species with senses that, with proper training, can enhance the work of law enforcement, fire investigators, and many other investigators. Dogs have an innate ability to understand the world through their senses in ways that are unavailable to us as humans. All trainers do in partnering with these four-legged detectives is work with them to channel their natural abilities toward tasks that help us do our jobs. Through consistent training, K9 trainers make dogs better at what they do. Crucially, trainers also learn to understand what dogs are communicating through their body language. They are the link between dogs and everyone else.

The canine–trainer partnership makes dogs a powerful and valuable tool. This is especially true because dogs never lie. A dog's body language always tells the truth, and as police officers, that body language can save lives, find contraband or dangerous substances, and be key in making our jobs safer.

Dogs can be applied in so many ways. When you are on an active call, and the suspect is gone when you arrive, the dog is your go-to solution. When you have a lost child who has wandered into the woods, the dog is your go-to solution. When you are searching for potentially hidden contraband, a possible explosive device, or the source of a fire due to suspected arson, the dog is your go-to solution. Take advantage of what dogs have to offer. It can mean the difference between life and death, or the difference between a suspect walking away from their crime and facing justice. Dogs help us do our jobs better; they are tools we can no longer do without.

Quick Reference Guides

Types of police service dogs

This short guide lays out the vocabulary typically used to refer to different types of dogs that may be used in police investigations. Remember that vocabulary, definitions, and training profiles differ from one jurisdiction to the next, and dogs may be trained in some of the skills listed below but not others. With standard and dual-purpose police service dogs in particular, be sure to confirm terms and training profiles with the K9 unit or units you work with so you know what skill sets are available to you.

TYPE OF DOG	COMMONLY TRAINED SKILLS
Standard police service dog *Common synonyms: patrol dog, utility dog*	• Tracking or trailing • Area search • Building search • Article search (evidence recovery) • Handler protection • Criminal apprehension
Dual-purpose police service dog	• Some or all standard police service dog skills • One detection profile
Search-and-rescue dog	• Tracking or trailing • Area search • Article search

TYPE OF DOG	COMMONLY TRAINED SKILLS
Single-purpose tracking dog	• Tracking only • Article search (evidence recovery)
Single-purpose trailing dog	• Trailing only • Article search (evidence recovery)
Single-purpose detector dog	• Detection only (one detection profile) • Profiles include: - Narcotics detection - Explosives detection - Accelerant detection - Human remains detection (HRD) - Wildlife detection

The right dog for the job

This reference guide is meant to give officers an idea of what type of dog to call in different situations. The table gives a number of generic example problems that officers are likely to encounter and suggests the best dog or dogs for the job.

PROBLEM	TYPE OF DOG TO CALL
You are searching for a person in a large area. You have identified a point last seen, but you do not need to prove where they came from. *Example: searching for a missing person who is not connected to crime.*	Police service dog or search-and-rescue dog trained in tracking, trailing, or area searches. *See **chapters 3** and **4**.*
You are searching for a person in a large area. You have identified a point last seen and you need to prove where the person came from. *Example: searching for a suspect who was last seen at a crime scene.*	Police service dog trained in tracking or trailing. *See **chapter 3**.*
You are searching for a person in a large area, but you have no source of track or point last seen.	Police service dog or search-and-rescue dog trained in area searches. *See **chapter 4**.*
You are searching for a person who is hiding inside a building.	Police service dog trained in building searches. *See **chapter 5**.*
You are searching for objects (evidence or lost articles) that have been handled by a person.	Police service dog trained in evidence recovery (also called article searches). *See **chapter 1**.*
You are searching for the remains of someone who is believed or known to be deceased.	Human remains detection (HRD) dog. *See **chapter 6**.*
You are searching for hidden narcotics.	Police service dog trained in narcotics detection. *See **chapter 6**.*

PROBLEM	TYPE OF DOG TO CALL
You are searching for hidden explosives.	Explosives detection dog. *See **chapter 6**.*
You are searching for evidence of accelerants. (Most often related to arson investigations.)	Accelerant detection dog. *See **chapter 6**.*
You are searching for the remains of poached or smuggled animals or animal remains.	Wildlife detection dog. *See **chapter 6**.*

Acknowledgments

Dr. Stephen Mackenzie (Doc) and I first met after reading each other's canine columns, which we shared in *Police Magazine* many decades ago. I reached out to him to assist me with a training problem and soon after found myself flying him out to Vancouver, BC, to give some hands-on training guidance to some teams I was working with at that time. After that, Steve and I began working together often. When he passed away unexpectedly, I lost a good friend and a generous mentor who taught me more about canine behavior and training techniques than anyone else. I continue to teach today what I learned from him. I have missed our jovial conversation and will be forever grateful for his friendship and mentorship over so many years.

Steve had just started rewriting this book when he passed away, and our publisher approached me to ask if I would be willing to finish what Steve started. I am honored and humbled to have been able to coauthor with Steve, and to help him to complete this work. While I have included updated techniques and written a significant amount of new material, I have also endeavored to try to keep the book in Steve's style, using as much of his original information as possible. This book is, first and foremost, Steve's creation and vision, and I am lucky to have had the chance to help him put it out in the world.

To those who provided photos—Billy Sawyer, Shelby Wright, Melinda Ruopp, David Ljunggren, and Erik Good—thank you!

To my daughter, Natasha Serena Eden, thank you for the time you put into the art concepts to help me get this across the finish line. To my wife, Natasha Eden, thank you for finalizing the figures for this book, and especially for your ongoing patience and support of my vision of making the law enforcement K9 world better. You've always been such a strong advocate for me. I'm blessed to have you in my life.

To my publishers, especially Kay Rollans, thank you for your patience. It seems there are never enough hours in my days, and you have always been more than patient with the deadlines. More importantly, thank you for trusting me with finishing Doc's book.

Finally, to Laurie and Dawn Mackenzie: Thank you for saying "yes" when I reached out to ask your permission to finish what Doc started. I hope it meets expectations.

With gratitude,
Robert S. Eden

About the Authors

Authors Stephen A. Mackenzie (left) and Robert S. Eden (right).

Dr. Stephen A. Mackenzie was a deputy sheriff for more than 20 years and trained and handled police service dogs for more than 30 years. A popular seminar instructor, he testified in both criminal and civil cases as a court-recognized expert in animal behavior. He was an integral part of the International Police K9 Conference, where he worked with thousands of police K9 teams over the years, and was a professor of animal science at the State University of New York at Cobleskill. Stephen passed away on March 22, 2021.

Robert S. Eden is a retired 28-year police veteran. Working with the Delta Police Department in British Columbia, Canada, Robert became a member of the dog section in 1983 and was appointed to the BC Police Commission's committee to create minimum police dog training standards for law enforcement agencies in the province. In 1991, he created and developed the International Police K9 Conference, a training seminar that was neither politically oriented nor specific to any particular style of training. Robert continues to consult worldwide on police K9 operations. He is also the creator of the K9 Activity Tracking System KATS Platinum, used by police agencies worldwide to maintain police dog training and deployment records, and is currently the CEO of Eden K9 Consulting & Training Corporation in Calgary, Alberta.